Teaching That Works

Teaching That Works

Effective Practice Combined with Theory and Research

Ann Chase

ROWMAN & LITTLEFIELD
Lanham • Boulder • New York • London

Published by Rowman & Littlefield
A wholly owned subsidiary of The Rowman & Littlefield Publishing Group, Inc.
4501 Forbes Boulevard, Suite 200, Lanham, Maryland 20706
www.rowman.com

Unit A, Whitacre Mews, 26-34 Stannary Street, London SE11 4AB

Copyright © 2016 by Ann Chase

All rights reserved. No part of this book may be reproduced in any form or by any electronic or mechanical means, including information storage and retrieval systems, without written permission from the publisher, except by a reviewer who may quote passages in a review.

British Library Cataloguing in Publication Information Available

Library of Congress Cataloging-in-Publication Data

Name: Chase, Ann, 1962–, author.
Title: Teaching that works : effective practice combined with theory and research / Ann Chase.
Description: Lanham : Rowman & Littlefield, [2016]
Identifiers: LCCN 2015045833| ISBN 9781475825930 (hardcover : alk. paper) | ISBN
    9781475825947 (pbk. : alk. paper)
Subjects: LCSH: Effective teaching. | School improvement programs.
Classification: LCC LB1025.3 .C417 2016 | DDC 371.102—dc23 LC record available at http://
    lccn.loc.gov/2015045833

∞ ™ The paper used in this publication meets the minimum requirements of American National Standard for Information Sciences Permanence of Paper for Printed Library Materials, ANSI/NISO Z39.48-1992.

Printed in the United States of America

To all those educators who still believe
we can change the world,
Yes We Can!

Contents

Preface		ix
Acknowledgments		xiii
Introduction		xv
1	Not Just Another School Improvement Book	1
2	Make Curriculum a Tool That Works	7
3	Instruction—Teaching That Works	17
4	Grades That Tell the Whole Story	29
5	Grading with Meaning	41
6	Testing to Get Real Results	53
7	Data Makes the Difference	63
8	Professional Development That Gets Results	73
9	Putting It All Together to Get Results	85
About the Author		93

Preface

Old, or should I say seasoned teachers, of whom I am now one, are fond of saying that there is nothing new in educational trends. I think that probably goes for most educational literature, as well.

Over the course of my career, I have read books on curriculum writing, books on educational strategies, books on classroom management, books on assessment, and the list goes on and on. If there is so much to be said about education and how to improve it, why do we have the feeling that we are still stuck in so many of the same old, bad habits? Why doesn't it get better?

Maybe the books are wrong. Maybe what the books tell us won't really work, or at least won't work in our schools. It could be that we educators are just buying the books and not reading them, but keeping them on the shelf to impress others. Maybe we just read and don't implement those great new suggestions. Education is complicated, and maybe there is no simple answer.

As a young teacher, and then a still young administrator, I still really thought I could I change the world. I began to realize that, from the assistant principal's office, I could have a unique view into the classroom through the eyes of the students. You see, when students are sent to the office, they tell you all kinds of things. They also give great insights into the instruction that is going on in classrooms, the delivery of that instruction, the management issues in the classroom, and the overall effectiveness of the classroom.

It turns out that students can be some of the best, most accurate observers of teacher behavior in the school. They have a much more thorough experience with the individual teachers in the building than the administrators. They also have a more detailed view of day-to-day instruction than any administrator could gain from a drop-in observation. The best part is that they will tell you all about what they see happening in the classroom.

This provides savvy administrators with the opportunity to be able to translate what students say into what is really going on in the classroom. It doesn't take much insight to figure out what has really happened in a classroom from the student's version of a story, provided you remember that students only tell stories from their own points of view. As an assistant principal, I discovered that I could then use what I learned about the conditions in the classroom to help teachers improve their classrooms.

Being an assistant principal afforded me the opportunity to attend conferences and workshops about the newest methodologies in professional development. It also gave me the opportunity to work closely with teachers, as an evaluator, and hopefully provide teachers with some strategies that would help both teachers and students.

I came to believe that we could profoundly change education. I believed then, and still do today, that some of the biggest impediments to success in schools are some of the practices we have inherited. If we could only stop for a few minutes and think through the way that we organize ourselves, magic could happen.

I worked closely with teachers in the area of professional development (PD) and was able to see the successes and failures of the PD programs that we, as a school, engaged in. I saw, firsthand, the disconnect between the good intentions of the PD programs that were offered and the lack of real change in some of our classrooms. In this position, I had the opportunity to help create the professional development that was implemented in our building.

After thirteen years as an administrator, circumstances changed and continuing to work in the building I was in was no longer an option. At this point, my life took a dramatic and unconventional turn. I decided that my passion would be more satisfied in the classroom than in chasing my administrative tail, and so I asked to be put back into the classroom. Imagine the surprise! Imagine the gossip! Administrators were sure I was giving up. Teachers were sure I was burned out.

What really happened was the realization, on my part, that I had a unique opportunity to put into practice all the innovations I had been trying to introduce to others. I could do more than just suggest to teachers that they try the methods I thought would work. I could prove those methods by doing it myself.

At this point you may be wondering why I am telling you my story instead of getting to the point. But the point is: Why are there so many books on improving education? And why does it seem that nothing ever changes?

For years, as an administrator, I believed that change was possible. Once I was back in a classroom, I actually had the chance to put my actions where my mouth was. It turns out that putting all the pieces in place, incorporating all that I had learned, does work! It really works! Not only that, but the kids like it, the parents like it, students are learning, and my principal is happy.

I feel that my own experience, as unorthodox as it has been, has provided me with unique insights. As a teacher the first time, I struggled to create an effective classroom with only my undergraduate training as a basis. I learned from my colleagues and from what I saw around me. I began to develop an idea of what I wanted my classroom to look like.

As an administrator, I had the opportunity to learn about the theories that underpin effective teaching. I attended conferences with members of the teaching staff and saw some of the best practices from districts around the country.

Being an administrator also gave me a student's-eye view into what happens in classrooms. It should come as no surprise that students are sent to the office much more frequently from ineffective classrooms than from effective classrooms. My desire to help students successfully navigate through their schooling led me to see, close up, the connection between school improvement and student achievement.

Not only was I exposed to best practices through my own study, I had the distance from the actual classroom to consider why some things worked and some other things did not. In the teacher evaluation process, I was able to have thoughtful conversations with teachers about what they were doing in their classrooms. I began to see which practices moved teachers forward and which practices were an impediment to student learning.

Now, as a classroom teacher again, I have embarked on the biggest action research project of all. Now that I have a better understanding of the theory behind effective schools, I can take the best practices and adapt them in ways that will really work from day to day. Since I know how the system works from both sides, I can take the best of all that I have learned and apply those ideas to my classroom simultaneously. I can integrate what I know about curriculum, instruction, grading, assessment, and data analysis in real time.

As I look back at my experience and the unusual perspective I have been granted of schools and teaching, I begin to think that perhaps I have something to offer to the wider world of education after all. I guess that, deep down, I do still think that we can change the world, and if not the whole world, then at least the everyday world of teachers and students.

This book is not a magic bullet. It is not a program. There is no one answer that will solve every problem, for every student, in every system, but I still believe that we can remake education for the better. We can have classrooms that work for students and for teachers. We can fix it!

Acknowledgments

With gratitude I would like to thank all of the people who have influenced my understanding of what it means to be a good teacher. I have been lucky to have worked with many dedicated and thoughtful people who have guided, supported, and encouraged my own work as an educator. Most especially I would like to thank Gabrielle Long, without whose encouragement I would never have attempted to write. Thanks, Gabbie, for being a sounding board and a proofreader.

Thanks to my family: my husband, Martin, who always supports me; my sons, Jason, Joe, and John, who have been my own personal action research projects; my lovely daughters-in-law, who cheer me on; and my precious grandchildren, who are just beginning the journey.

Last but not least, thank you to Rowman & Littlefield for taking a chance on an unknown.

Introduction

This book is intended to fill a rather large gap in the educational literature available to teachers. It is not a scholarly book of research. It is not a magic program that will instantly create a high-performing school. Instead, this is a practical book for teachers who are hard at work every day trying to improve.

A quick review of the existing literature will show that for all of the material that is available to teachers, very little if any considers all of the major functions of teaching in a manageable way.

This seems to be a rather glaring omission. It assumes that teachers have the time, not to mention the expertise, to gather all of the best practices together and simultaneously integrate them into a meaningful flow. Good teaching encompasses everything from curriculum development to assessment with a healthy dose of data analysis, but do practicing teachers have a clear understanding of how to weave the pieces together?

What many teachers need is a simple, comprehensive look at each of the components of what makes a successful classroom and what ties those individual components into a rational whole. How does the theory inform the practice? How do busy teachers take all the professional development pieces and use them simultaneously?

This book has two major goals: first, to translate the theory behind all of the research-based best practices that teachers have been taught into practical language that teachers can use in their classrooms, and second, to bring together all of the seemingly disparate components of teaching into a meaningful whole.

Theory without practical application is not useful to most teachers. Teachers have a lot on their plates in this era of increased scrutiny, when accountability and high-stakes tests have transformed the landscape of schools. Although the research into best practices has never been better, working classroom teachers often find it difficult to translate that research into day-to-day practice.

Teacher professional development, although well-intentioned, does not necessarily help. The current emphasis on research-based methods has created a fragmented and piecemeal approach to school improvement. Each new study of one of the components of teaching leads to an emphasis on that one component. From curriculum to instruction, grading practices, and data analysis, in-service learning has the feel of a book-of-the-month club, with no focus in any one direction.

Just as groups of like-minded individuals working together can generate a synergy that makes the whole greater than the sum of its parts, creating a classroom that effectively blends all of the major components of teaching into a unified whole makes learning more robust. If teachers are going to meet the demands that the twenty-first century requires, it will be from harnessing this synergy in their teaching.

Each chapter in this book takes apart one of the major components of teaching. Beginning with curriculum and moving through instruction, grading, and data analysis, the pieces that go into effective teaching are examined, beginning with a description of some of the most current practices and challenges that educators face.

First comes a description of the conditions that teachers face on a day-to-day basis, then a look at the theory that should guide good practice. The demands on classrooms have never been greater, and so it has never been more important for teachers to stop and consider what current research into best practices has to say. Too often, research is presented in a format that, while conducive to the methods of research, is too tightly packed for immediate use in the classroom. This work is intended to be a straightforward presentation of the research.

In keeping with a straightforward treatment of each component, there are practical examples of ways that teachers can apply best practice in their daily teaching and routines. Often the application of research has been presented in a cumbersome or burdensome way, which does not have to be the case. Reworking traditional methods can be not only more effective but also less labor-intensive.

Finally, each chapter contains examples and anecdotes taken from the day-to-day experiences of teachers who have adapted their instruction in ways that illustrate the application of these best practices and research-based theories. These are not meant to be all-inclusive, nor are they step-by-step instructions. These examples are meant to take the generic language of theory and make it accessible for day-to-day use.

Each chapter concludes with a list of the key points from the chapter. These key points can provide a focus for professional conversations that both lead to a reexamination of current practice and set out a framework for moving forward to a classroom that gets results.

This is not a book of breakthrough theories and ideas. Nothing that is contained here is different from what is set forth in numerous other works designed to improve classrooms and schools and to boost student achievement. What is unique about this treatment is the holistic nature of the presentation. Too much of the material designed to help teachers has the opposite effect.

The fragmented nature of school improvement literature has left teachers feeling overwhelmed and pulled in different directions. Just as soon as one improvement initiative has begun to take root, it is replaced by another. Stepping back and considering all of the major steps in the teaching process can lead to refocusing on student learning and harnessing the power of synergy—truly leading to classrooms that work, both for teachers and their students.

Chapter One

Not Just Another School Improvement Book

Much of the literature on education, and certainly on educational improvement, is written by researchers. This is as it should be. Researchers spend years studying and testing various methodologies. Therein often lies the very reason that this methodology has not been widely integrated into classrooms: It takes years of specific study.

Most teachers don't have the time, not to mention the luxury, of focusing on just one aspect of education. They have to juggle all the balls at once. Classroom teachers can't spend all their time just on curriculum, or focus only on teaching strategies, because there are still assessments to worry about, grades to track, and on and on.

Researchers, on the other hand, have an understandably narrow focus. By its very nature, research is specific and directed at a specific topic in the realm of teaching. There is excellent research available in the areas of curriculum, teaching strategies, formative and summative assessment, data-driven instruction, and so forth. The challenge for classroom teachers, and for professional development planners, is integrating all the research into what happens in classrooms on a day-to-day basis.

In addition to books on research, many other books are written by those who long ago left the classroom and now spend their time speaking and writing about ways to improve education. These efforts are also worthy. Successful educators take the strategies and methods they have perfected and turn them into programs designed to be replicated by others. But very often these programs are just that: programs.

One of the reasons so many of these kinds of resources are not as helpful as teachers would like is because they are used in one of two ways: as idiot guides or as canned programs. This is not to say that the goal of these educators is to have their successful programs distorted in such ways, but inept professional development often does just that.

Start with idiot guides. Does anyone really think that the essence of good teaching can be distilled into a potion that can be fed to an idiot? One should hope not! Teaching is complicated. It has more moving parts than the most complex piece of machinery. It changes from year to year, from class to class, and even from day to day depending on the mix of students in the room. Once good teaching has been distilled down to its elemental parts, all that is left is the parts without the addition of a skilled professional.

Trying to construct a classroom like a paint-by-number set is an exercise in futility. There are just too many uncontrollable variables in any classroom to make step-by-step instructions viable.

Then consider the other possible use of an idiot guide. Does anyone want an idiot in the classroom teaching students? If any kind of person can be brought in off of the street and given a document that will allow them to successfully teach living, breathing young people, what does that say about what is expected of teachers?

It has been said that classroom teachers are second only to air traffic controllers in the number of decisions they make in a day. That may or may not be true, but just think about the number of decisions the average teacher makes in a day.

What could be so seemingly simple as a student request to use the restroom? Any veteran teacher can tick off the perils hidden in this simple request. In an instant the teacher must weigh and consider the following questions.

- What is the school policy on students in the hall?
- What is this student's history in unsupervised settings?
- Does he have an IEP, 504, or medical plan that requires he be given unlimited access to restroom breaks?
- If this student is allowed to leave the room, who will ask next?
- How many times has this student asked to leave in the middle of class in the past few weeks?
- Have there been any incidents in the restroom down the hall? Smoking? Vandalism?
- When is this period scheduled to end, and can she wait until class is over?
- What instruction is he going to miss while he is gone?
- What was the content of the last conversation with her parent?

Most teachers could probably add to this list. If a request as simple as a student asking to use the restroom creates such a lengthy set of questions, what about the important stuff? What kinds of decisions do teachers need to make in regard to what to teach? How to teach? Assessments? State test scores?

There is no reasonable way at all to so simplify the job of teaching so as to "idiot-proof" it. What is more, should any child be in an "idiot's" classroom? Would anyone want their child to be in that teacher's classroom?

The other and even more insidious problem is the "canned program." What is this? The superintendent, assistant superintendent, principal, assistant principal, or instructional coach goes to a conference or reads a book. He returns to the school with an award-winning program that turned around another school and made that school the envy of every district in a three-state area.

That leader (the superintendent, assistant superintendent, or principal) is now going to plop that program into his own school system and make the same kind of gains. This may sound like a good idea, but does it work?

A perfect example of this phenomenon was a bestseller some years back. *Fish: A Remarkable Way to Boost Morale and Improve Results*, by Stephen C. Lundin, Ph.D., Harry Paul, and John Christensen, is a book not even specifically aimed at education. It is a wonderful story of how a fish market in Seattle turned their business into a bona-fide tourist attraction. One of the most memorable lines was something to the effect that if a fish market can be a fun place to work, any place can become a fun place to work.

The company spent a year imagining what it could be as a company, defining their beliefs and acting on them, and then they wrote a book. Walking into a school not long after the publication of this book, one could tell immediately whether or not the staff had read the *Fish* book. How? If they had, there would be fish taped up to the walls, hanging from the ceiling, incorporated into the stationery; fish would be everywhere.

It was equally apparent that the leaders in that building didn't get it. The point of the book was not about the fish; rather, the book was the story of how to make an organization a fun and vibrant place to work while maintaining the integrity of the mission.

As happens with every other program, after a little while the fish came down off the wall. Why? Because it was a "program." Educators love programs. Everybody wants a shortcut. Just tell them what to do and they will follow a model and the model will solve all their problems.

This will never work! No matter how great a program may work in another school, it can never be plopped into a different random school and achieve the same results. Why?

Go all the way back to the earliest research on effective schools. One of the earliest descriptors of effective schools was that they had high expectations, commonly shared. Interestingly enough, an examination of the history of effective schools shows that this same descriptor, or one very much like it, appears on every effective schools research list.

Why did *Fish* work? Because the people at the fish market spent lots of time, and even more conversation, about what they wanted, what they had, and how it could be better. They did not just adopt another company's program; they created their own—one that would meet the needs that they had identified as being important.

Why didn't reading the book change most of the schools that had fish hanging from the rafters? Simple: They hung fish from the rafters! For too many people, the whole point of implementing a canned program is so that they don't have to "waste all that time" developing something from scratch. It cuts out all those meetings.

People hate meetings. Leaders everywhere, in all sorts of businesses, do everything they can to avoid meetings. Disdain for meetings has become the required response to the very word. Meetings are the enemy. It just so happens that, in point of fact, meetings may not be the problem. Perhaps it is just bad meetings that are bad.

Meetings that allow for a greater understanding of the goal of the organization are actually what makes most programs successful. Remember that one of the first indicators of an effective school is high expectations that are commonly shared. One of the best ways to commonly share anything is to sit down and talk about it. It is for this reason that a school could adopt a "Pizza on Tuesdays" program and have tremendous success!

What? How could "Pizza on Tuesdays" change anything? What is "Pizza on Tuesdays" anyway? The answer is simple. There actually is no such thing, but if a school spent enough time with the teachers, administrators, parents, and (add a favorite stakeholder group here), developing "Pizza on Tuesdays," talking about how it would improve achievement, attendance, morale, and (pick a favorite target), it would work.

Why would "Pizza on Tuesdays" work? Not because of the pizza, not because of the choice of Tuesdays, but because of the conversation. It would improve the school because the right group of thoughtful, caring people spent enough time talking about what they wanted and how they were going to get there.

This book is not intended to be an idiot's guide; it is not a canned program. It is a synthesis of things that good teachers already know. The difference between this book and most of the other school-improvement books on the market is that this book looks at (or at least attempts to look at) the whole enchilada: not just one piece of the complicated dance that teachers do, but a look at the whole picture.

Synergy is a powerful concept, and it is one of the desired outcomes of meetings. Synergy is the idea that the whole is greater than the sum of the parts. This concept is certainly one of the components of a good meeting.

If synergy comes from working in a group, if two heads really are better than one, think what can be accomplished if all the parts of teaching are examined, and then put into practice, as a whole. If all the working parts actually worked together, toward the same end, what kind of results could be achieved?

Teaching is not just the curriculum. It is not just the instruction that the teacher provides. Teaching is a combination of curriculum and instruction with effective feedback and data analysis. There are many parts to teaching, but most of the material that exists to help teachers improve only addresses the components of teaching one at a time.

Likewise, effective classrooms are a combination of theory and practice. Effective practices are always supported by sound theory. What happens to the average classroom teacher is that they don't have the time or the training to translate the research and theory into actual "kids in the room," day-to-day practice.

By putting the theory and research together with the practice in a way that gets teachers thinking about what they do and why they do it, maybe education can move beyond the frustration. Teachers may be tired of hearing about the newest, latest, greatest methods. They may be tired of professional learning that seems like just another way to fill up a Professional Development Day, but they are not tired of trying to improve what they do.

Teachers want students to be successful—all of them. School can be better than it is, if those who teach can just put the right pieces together. All of the pieces—curriculum, instruction, grading, and data analysis—can be put together in a way that makes the final product more than just the sum of its parts.

KEY IDEAS TO REMEMBER

- Good teaching is a job for professionals and cannot, should not, be reduced to a step-by-step set of instructions.
- There is no substitute for real, genuine conversation between professionals about expectations, and those conversations should take time to be meaningful.
- Meetings are not the enemy; bad meetings are the enemy. Stay focused on the goal and let the details evolve from there.
- Good teaching is more than a sum of the parts of good teaching. It is not enough to improve just one component of teaching (i.e., curriculum, instruction, assessment, etc.). All of the components need to support each other.
- Sound educational theory should be the basis of good practice. Knowing why a strategy works makes the implementation of the strategy more effective.

QUESTIONS FOR FURTHER REFLECTION

- What do you see as the strengths of your classroom/school? What are the areas that most need improvement?
- In what ways do you achieve synergy in your work? How would increased cooperation between the components of your work increase your effectiveness?

Chapter Two

Make Curriculum a Tool That Works

If the goal is to watch teachers groan and roll their eyes at a professional development event, start with the word *curriculum*. It's not that teachers don't care about what they teach; on the contrary, most teachers are very passionate about what they teach. Secondary teachers often get into teaching for that very reason, and they consider themselves experts in their content area. No, what makes teachers tired is the endless contortions they feel they make with regard to written curriculum and the ways that curriculum is developed and adopted.

Sadly, many teachers view curriculum as an extra burden added to an already exhausting load, or as just another state mandate that will shift as soon as the political wind changes direction. To those who feel this way about curriculum, suspend the skepticism for a moment and consider the possibility that the problem is not curriculum. Perhaps the problem stems from the way that curriculum is used on a day-to-day basis.

In today's schools, nearly all teachers are provided with a school board–approved curriculum document. This may have been developed by teachers in the district, by the state, or by an outside company. No matter where it comes from, however, all too often it is an empty document that sits in a binder on a teacher's shelf, or even more sadly, in the library, where it serves no purpose other than to meet state requirements.

Many of these documents deserve the respect they get (which is none at all). Too often they are written to satisfy guidelines or standards and are not written to help or guide teachers. What is even worse is that sometimes these documents are so convoluted that they make it harder rather than easier for a teacher to teach.

If teachers have a good curriculum in place, or even better, one that they helped to write themselves *and* that they use, hooray! That classroom is headed in a good direction. But there is almost no chance that a teacher will be successful in teaching, or that students will be successful in learning, if the teacher doesn't have a clear idea of what it is that they are trying to teach.

If there is no curriculum, or if the document provided by the district is poorly written, don't fear. A useful curriculum doesn't have to be a monstrously long, complex document in order to be successful. As a matter of fact, too much can be just as bad as not enough. It turns out that the most important part of the exercise in writing curriculum is thinking through what to teach. Formatting an official document is most definitely a secondary concern.

At this point of the process, it is important to make a distinction with which some readers will certainly disagree. Exactly what is contained in the curriculum document, and how it is formatted, is not nearly as important as it is sometimes made out to be. Following the official, written curriculum to the letter is not the mark of an effective teacher. Maybe students don't really have to memorize every factoid included in the curriculum document.

Before this idea is rejected out of hand as blasphemy, consider this. Schools are no longer in the business of just teaching facts; they can't be. Once computers brought the Internet, and its endless supply of information, into the classroom, the business of facts was dead. This certainly does not mean that facts don't matter. However, the days when facts were a finite set of information that could be contained in a book, memorized, and then regurgitated are over.

This is not a bad thing. Most teachers have spent a good deal of time in classrooms—elementary school, high school, and college classrooms—where the requirement was simply to memorize information. This memorized material was then promptly forgotten as soon as the test was turned in. This was not a good way to learn then, but it is an impossibility now. There is now no end to the number of facts available at the touch of a keypad. And if this is true, then what facts should be taught?

Go one step further. Should schools ever have been fixated on facts in the first place? Instead, shouldn't schools focus on how to access information and what students should do with the information once it has been acquired? If educators accept this as true, that the *why* and *how* are more important than the *what*, then how does any teacher know what to teach?

How about the state and national standards? After all, if that is what THE TEST is going to address, why not teach it?

Listen to the gasps of horror! Teach to the test? Shocking! How could someone else, someone who often is not even an educator, decide what should be taught in the classroom? Isn't teaching to the test actually cheating?

Okay, so maybe this is an exaggeration, but if teachers are honest, they will all admit that they have at least heard this argument before. Teaching to the test has gotten a bad rap; follow the argument and it makes even less sense. What a rejection of teaching to the test is really saying is this: Let's not tell the kids what they are supposed to know. Instead, let's make them guess, and then complain when they don't get it.

Teaching to the test is really more a complaint about the test than it is about the teaching. If students are given an objective test and are just memorizing responses, not even facts, but just answers, then *of course* teaching what is *on* the test is foolishness (or even cheating). On the other hand, teaching students the *information* that is being tested seems to be simple common sense. More on testing later.

In the effort to defend schools from the mediocrity that some see as a result of state testing, and to raise standards, those who argue against teaching to the test have forgotten a basic truth. The need to teach students the material, the information they need to know, which is what is being tested, is obvious.

If it is so obvious, then why do so many teachers have trouble articulating what they want students to know? The answer: the curriculum. So many of the curriculum documents used in schools are written so densely, are packed with so many objectives, have so much information in them, that they are not user-friendly. That is a real shame, because those documents are given to new teachers with the belief that those new teachers, armed with their curriculum documents, should then be fully equipped to go into the classroom and teach, make a difference, change the world!

Ideally, teachers work through curriculum documents with other teachers in their departments and schools. Working collaboratively with the other teachers in the building or even in the district is definitely the most powerful way to develop curriculum tools that can actually be of use. If working collaboratively is not possible, all is not lost; individual teachers can still rework a curriculum document that is already in place and make it work for them rather than against them.

A note of caution: This is not to recommend, nor even suggest, that teachers ignore the curriculum document they have been given. In almost all cases, this is the document that has been approved by the school board. Teachers are hired, by that school board, to teach what that board has mandated, and it is a contractual obligation to do so.

What is being recommended is that teachers do more than just read through the curriculum document. Do more than just use the curriculum as a paperweight. To really teach, and to have students learn what is contained within those documents, it is necessary to have a thorough knowledge of what is written there.

Effective teachers know the order in which the material needs to be presented to students, and the depth with which it needs to be taught. To be effective means to be familiar with what is contained in the curriculum. This level of familiarity only comes from actually writing the document or from taking the thing apart and putting it back together.

Important note: The textbook is *not* the same as the curriculum. Go ahead and use the textbook as a reference when developing personal outlines or guides, but using the text as a direct teaching guide all too often results in proctoring and not teaching.

Consider this: If anyone, someone off the street, can come into a classroom, use the textbook teacher's guide, and successfully educate students, then why do schools need professional teachers or teacher education? Teachers are not just random individuals picked out of a hat, and the act of teaching cannot, nor should not, be made "idiot-proof." Slavishly following a textbook teacher's guide is more like proctoring than teaching.

Textbooks are, by their nature, created for use by anyone. The thinking behind textbooks seems to be to allow for any individual to be able to come in off the street and use the materials. Using the textbook as a substitute for curriculum or as the only source of information for students, results in classrooms that are really boring.

Yes, there are enough worksheets, which come in the big box with the new textbooks when they are adopted, to keep the students busy all year. Tests are already there for instant reproduction, but simple ease of use is not what education is all about. If the task at hand is to educate students, to prepare them for the future, and yes, to have them successfully score well on the standardized tests, teachers must be much more than proctors.

Creating a classroom that works means that teachers have used the written curriculum to develop their own personal plan or guide, which should drive instruction. This plan will literally be a guide to the everyday work. How does a teacher go about developing a personal outline?

Start with identifying the scope of the material that is to be addressed over the course of the year. This sounds obvious, but a clear understanding, in a big-picture way, of where to start, what to cover, and where to stop is critical to being able to address those areas and not meander all around the globe.

Once a clear idea of the starting and ending places in the curriculum is identified, develop the units, or big chunks that the material falls into. Any reasonable curriculum should logically have the units that are to be taught explicitly defined, but it is amazing how often this is not true.

An example: Many schools have a curriculum for American History that is written in strands: economics, citizenship, geography, history, etc. Organizing the objectives that are important for students to know in this way may be reasonable. Indeed, the national standards for the teaching of Social Studies are written this way. But teaching a class of students in this format is most certainly not reasonable!

Imagine teaching all about the economics of American History from colonization to the present, and then going back and teaching about the geography of America. Then go back again and teach what it means to be a citizen, and on through seven different and discrete standards. The students would be so confused and lost they would have no clear idea about the storyline that is our nation's history.

If the current curriculum guide is organized in any way other than with the chunking and sequencing that present a logical progression one would use to actually teach students, then it is absolutely necessary for the teacher to rearrange those objectives in order to create a personal outline that can be used to guide lessons. This personal outline should still include the required material, but it should be organized in such a way that it provides the teacher with a framework that makes sense.

How does an individual teacher know what units to create? It is easy to assume that all teachers are experts in their content areas; in fact, this is often the case, and it is certainly most desirable. Sadly, because of variations in certification criteria, what is desirable is not always true. All too often, teachers are assigned to positions that are not in their primary area of certification. Unfortunately, in a climate of budgetary constraints, money drives the way teaching assignments are made instead of the teacher's expertise in that subject serving as the driver.

If a teacher is assigned to teach a specific course as a content expert, arranging material into logical chunks or units is relatively easy. If that is not the case, being assigned to teach a course in which the teacher's content knowledge is limited can create panic. By all means, those teachers should look at textbooks, published curriculum, and websites for guidance. Use common sense about the material. In what order does it make sense? Does the material build on itself, or is it chronological? Think about ordering the material in the way in which it would make sense if it were being introduced for the first time.

Units should be relatively broad and non-specific. A general rule of thumb is from three to five units a semester. If a summative assessment is to be given at the end of each unit, a few more units may be in order. If summative assessments are planned more often throughout the unit, the units can be fewer. Keep the amount of new material covered on each assessment to a reasonable level for the grade. If there is so much material that the summative assessment becomes overwhelming, break the material into smaller pieces.

Remember, the goal is to chunk the material for students. Find the natural breaks, or the themes, or concepts in the material. The more logical the development of the units, the easier it will be for students to make sense of what is being taught. Providing students with a framework for understanding is critical.

Young people are already expected to juggle many different content areas at one time. If they aren't provided with some logical way to organize the material, it becomes a jumbled mess, which ends in frustration for both teacher and student.

Think about it: Students are asked, in effect, to be actively reading from five to eight different subjects (think books) at the same time and are expected to master them all. Imagine if teachers were asked to read even more than three books simultaneously and then were tested on the material! There would be outrage! Grievances would be filed! Yet schools ask the same thing of young people without a second thought.

The only way students can reasonably be expected to effectively learn and, more importantly, retain the information that is taught, is to make that information as logical and organized as possible. Not only should it be organized and logical, but students need to be taught the relationships between the facts, not merely the facts themselves.

The more connections that students make between the ideas that they are exposed to, the more real learning takes place. Brain research informs this idea. New information is categorized by the brain alongside existing information. If students are expected to learn random facts about a topic, chances are those unrelated facts will be quickly lost.

Once the units are organized, it's time to develop objectives or learning targets. Unit by unit, think about what students should know and be able to do in relation to the specific standards. These objectives should also be relatively broad, not lists of factoids.

Objectives go by a wide variety of names: essential learning outcomes, enduring understandings, big ideas, learning targets, etc. All of these names work. It's not the nomenclature that is important; rather, think about objectives as literally what students really *need to know* about this topic and what they should be able *to actually do* to demonstrate they know it. Keep this list at a manageable number; eight to ten per summative assessment is a good target. Too many and the task becomes too big for both the teacher to assess and the student to learn.

This is a good time to review a really important idea that can be extremely hard for teachers to embrace. Classroom teachers often know so much about their subject and they can be so passionate about it that they want to share all that wonderful knowledge. Listen carefully: *No one can teach it all!* There is no way. No one learned all they know about any one topic in a single sitting, and neither can your students.

The ability, and what is more, the willingness on the part of teachers to be selective and reasonable about what is taught and what students are expected to retain is so important. Too many teachers beat themselves up over this. (And too many curriculum guides expect it!) Trying to teach it all is setting both teacher and students up for a fall. Either the concepts will be "covered" so quickly that students will not have a genuine understanding, or the end of the year will arrive before all of the objectives are met.

The ability, and the permission, to make decisions about the work that goes on from day to day is the mark of a professional. Teachers are professionals, and as such they need to employ their training to determine what information is critical for students to master and which information is simply enrichment. The critical information becomes the focus of the objectives.

Back to objectives: How are those eight to ten objectives developed? Go back to the standards that are published. If the course that is being taught is an area that is tested, by all means, focus on those areas. If the course is not a tested area, look to the district or state curriculum guide or go to the website for the national organization. Every content area has a national organization that has already identified the specific body of knowledge for that discipline.

In either case, it is likely that no single course will be able to realistically cover all the areas that are listed. Be smart; look for those ideas that will give the most bang for the buck. What eight to ten items will yield the maximum "points" on the test? Even in tested areas, all of the expectations listed in the curriculum are not equal. Every test has its limits. Research the expectations that account for the greatest number of points. These are nearly always the ones that are a natural focus anyway.

Be realistic. If no one can teach it all, and teachers, schools, and students are going to be held accountable on high-stakes tests, then classroom time needs to be spent doing what will yield the greatest benefit. This is merely good time management.

This is the point at which many teachers break out into hives. How can an individual teacher make the decision to "leave out" material? What will happen if every single item listed in every single curriculum document is not covered? Administrators reading this book and asking this question may not like the answer. The simple truth is this, *No one can teach it all.* No one can! Those who try will end up teaching lots of stuff, but students will really learn only a little.

A story to illustrate this point: There once was a very wise teacher. He was a department chair at a large suburban high school and was also an adjunct professor of teaching methods at a highly respected private university. During one of the first class sessions at the university, he would give his pre-service teachers a textbook and a calendar. The task he assigned them was to map out how they would teach that course in the days allotted by the school calendar.

His students would typically do what too many teachers try to do. They started on day one with chapter 1, section 1. On day two they taught section 2, then section 3, and so on until they reached the end of the chapter, and then they gave a test. The pre-service teachers quickly realized that they would run out of school year before they ran out of textbook.

If this is the case, there are only two options: Teach right up to the end of the year and only cover what was covered, or make a choice about what to leave out in the middle. Be sure of one thing: Something will have to be sacrificed. The question becomes this: Is the professional educator in the classroom going to decide what is less important and can be skipped over, or is the calendar going to decide that what is at the end of the curriculum document is the least important part of the material?

Every teacher faces the same dilemma as those pre-service teachers: What to leave out? It shouldn't take long to decide. If both teacher and student are going to be held accountable for student scores on standardized state tests, and students are going to carry the results of those tests as a part of their permanent record, then some judicious pruning of material is in order. Teachers are obligated to do everything they can to make those scores the best they can be.

The flipside of this line of reasoning may hurt some feelings. If some things are already being "left out" because of time constraints, it is going to be hard to justify "leaving in" pet topics, objectives, or units if they are not part of the required material. The days when a teacher could spend large chunks of time teaching their pet projects are over.

This does not mean that teachers cannot or should not share their passions with their students. It is important to show students that the topics being taught are genuinely interesting. If the instructor is not interested in the material, why should the student be? Those areas of high interest to teachers often intrigue students, as well, and demonstrate that the subject is genuinely interesting to others and can be interesting to them too. What schools no longer can afford to do, however, is spend large chunks of time on areas that are not critical to success in meeting standards.

Formal curriculum documents are only a beginning. Yes, there is an obligation to use the documents that have been approved by the school board, but that does not mean that those documents are necessarily appropriate to use exactly as they are written. Neither can a textbook be an absolute road map to lesson planning.

Knowing what to teach is where every teacher needs to start. If the person in charge of the classroom doesn't have a clear idea of what is important, what students should know, and what students should be able to do, then there will be no effective lessons, assessments, grades, or any other components of good classrooms.

Start with the big ideas and work down to the individual pieces that are critical to student understanding. Use those state and local standards; don't fight against them. Sometimes leaning into the resistance is not only easier, but in the end it can result in much less grief.

Although most curriculum guides are developed for direct and immediate use by teachers, the truth is that it just isn't always that easy. Teachers who rely only on district or state curriculum guides are banking on a false economy. The time that is saved in pre-planning will most certainly be spent later on in the year. Teachers who don't have a clear and workable plan to address all of the major curriculum goals in a logical way will be scrambling to finish in the end.

When each teacher creates a personal outline that delineates the scope of the course, the main ideas or units to be taught, and the individual objectives, the first step to moving away from one-size-fits-all teaching is made.

One more step remains after creating this outline. Teachers need to take a realistic look at the end of the year, before school even starts. Teaching is rather unique in that it has a clearly defined beginning and end. A new group of students comes in at the beginning, and they leave at the end. Whether they have learned it or not, in most cases, at the end of the year they are done.

This means that teachers need to have a clear sense of the passage of time. It would be safe to say that the norm for most teachers in the past was to teach up to the end, and what was covered was what was covered. Case in point, the vast majority of history students can relate that they never got to the present day in their coursework.

This is no longer acceptable, if it ever was. If students and teachers are accountable for a predetermined set of content knowledge, then the teacher is obligated to make sure that the material is at least addressed before the students take the high-stakes test. Add to this the reality that the state tests are rarely given at the very end of the year, but in many cases a month or more before the scheduled last day of school.

The only way for a teacher to have any confidence that he will address all of the critical content in the time allotted is to plan for it. Now every teacher, or almost every teacher, plans. However, too many teachers have fallen into the habit of planning in the short term and completely ignoring the long term. It was common for teachers to think of planning as one unit at a time and then, when the end of the school year arrived, the learning was ended, too.

Once a teacher has developed a personal outline for their curriculum, it is a relatively easy next step to put that document next to the calendar and make the outline fit into the days allotted. The easiest way to start this process is also the simplest. If units are relatively equal in the number of objectives, and they should be, count the number of units to be covered during the year. Count the actual weeks of school (take out all the days that are already scheduled off), and divide by the number of units.

This may not be the exact length of each unit—that can be adjusted as needed—but it is a good place to start. How much time does that leave in each unit and for each objective? This can be the best tool for deciding what information can be considered enrichment and which is critical. Time is a constant in school, not a variable. The only way to make sure that the most important curricular objectives are addressed is by deliberately planning.

The work of creating a curriculum map, pacing guide, semester calendar, etc., is so often overlooked by classroom teachers. Many times, teachers who are already busy see these tools as just one more burden. In reality, creating a realistic plan to address all of the important objectives can save time and panic later in the school year.

Even at the beginning of this process of looking at teaching as a whole, it is easy to see the interrelatedness of the various parts. What students should know is dictated by the curriculum, which is integral to teacher planning. These two components do not exist as separate considerations. As more components are added, the synergy between them grows.

To really fix what is broken in schools and make classrooms that work, thinking of curriculum as a tool that can be employed by each teacher in each classroom to guide the learning is a natural place to start. Curriculum is more than just a document, and effective teachers know how to use curriculum as a tool that puts them in control of the learning.

KEY IDEAS TO REMEMBER

- Good curriculum is foundational to effective teaching.
- Curriculum is more than the official curriculum documents. Teachers need to have, or develop, a guide that gives clear direction on what is to be taught and why it is important.
- Teacher guides need to be developed by the teacher and organized into meaningful and logical "chunks," or units. Assessments will be designed around these units.
- Work smarter, not harder. Focus objectives on the items that yield the most "points" on the state assessment.
- Plan ahead. The school year contains a finite number of days, and the key objectives must be taught in that time.

QUESTIONS FOR FURTHER REFLECTION

- How do you, as a teacher, use written curriculum in your teaching?
- Have you as a teacher, or as a building, examined the state standards to determine which curricular objectives carry the most weight in each course? How do you address these standards differently from the other standards in your district curriculum?
- What long-range planning do you do in your classroom/school? Do you create a curriculum map or pacing guide? How might you use such a plan in your instruction?

Chapter Three

Instruction — Teaching That Works

Once the curriculum guide, the state and district standards, and/or the national association guidelines are put into a personal outline, an effective road map has been developed for teaching the specific course. Now it is time to go in and deliver the content to the students. This is the public part of teaching, AND it is almost always one of the components educators are most judged on. When teachers are observed and evaluated, it is most typically on their actual teaching with students in the room.

Not only is formal evaluation based most closely on this area, but this is where the "rubber meets the road." This is what students see, and this environment is where they spend most of their waking hours. Instruction is the area that many teacher resources most closely attend to.

Unfortunately, there is a distracting new and growing trend, not just in education but in the private sector, as well—a premise that seems to have been adopted by so many educators. It seems that every time someone wants to improve their organization, they feel they have to change the terminology. Keep the same old practices in place, just call it by new name. Repackage it and try it again. It's as if somehow, by simply changing what something is called, it will automatically be performed with more skill and determination.

It all too often seems that if an initiative or program is not working, those in charge think that if they just change the name (and change the forms), people will somehow magically understand the goal and be able to achieve it. Somehow everyone has the idea that if the current practice is not working, it is not the fault of the practice itself, but rather because there is an unclear name attached to the program.

Although this description is overly simplistic, it resonates. The sad thing is that it is easy to sympathize with the motive. Changing the name is easy; it requires *no real* change in behavior. And after all, everyone wants the words they use to communicate the ideas they embrace; words matter. It's not easy to do this job, and it is even harder if the goal continues to be elusive. When people are already working hard, it is easy for them to believe that the problem is one of understanding the intent, not a failure of the program that is in place.

As a result, there is a seemingly endless supply of "new" teaching strategies. Teachers are left with the idea that student achievement will skyrocket if they will just use the newest, latest strategy. All too often, those teachers who are less than effective in the first place are the ones who are encouraged to use the "new" strategy. It should not come as a shock that an ineffective teacher very well may still be ineffective even with a great new strategy.

The trend to rebrand only makes the problem worse. Teachers who have been in the game long enough see the latest and greatest come back into vogue. It is no wonder that those teachers, especially the ones who struggle, eventually face each new strategy with skepticism. Their assumption of the failure of the strategy becomes a self-fulfilling prophecy.

To really get a handle on what it means to be a good teacher, it is important to spend some time on philosophy. All of this is an attempt to ease into a discussion of the difference between teaching and learning. Oh, are there groans again? People have heard this before. Obviously teaching happens so that learning happens; what does everyone think teachers are doing behind those doors? Teaching and learning are the same thing, right?

Okay, think about the implications. If teaching is happening without a clear focus on learning, then that is exactly what does happen. Teaching without learning. Teachers might as well be teaching to the wall if students are not being impacted. And sometimes even the very best teachers feel that is exactly what they are doing some days anyway: teaching to the wall.

So often, the simplest, most obvious details are the very ones that can reinvigorate and get the train back on the track. The connection between teaching and learning is just such a detail. Just because teaching is happening, it should not be a given that learning is also happening.

Teaching, as a concept in isolation, can all too easily become an uninspired recitation of facts to students, who are, or quickly become, unengaged and disinterested. It becomes mechanical and boring to both the students and the teacher. Learning, on the other hand, is an exciting exercise that really never gets old. No matter what age, educational level, socioeconomic class, gender, or race we are, learning really can be fun.

Consider this: If learning was not intrinsically engaging, would commercial television be willing to devote so much time to programming that is educational in nature? If "non-educator" adults, who can choose what they spend their time and money on, still choose to watch programming that teaches them something about themselves and their world, why do teachers have to work so hard to get young people to play along? The answer, in too many cases, is because the adults in the classroom are so busy "teaching" that there is little time or thought given to "learning." More on this in a little while.

A related topic, and the one that is the most critical distinction that teachers should make, is the difference between on-task behavior and student engagement. Here is a place where the words really do matter. When considering student engagement, this most emphatically *does not* simply mean students who are merely on task. These two things, *on task* and *engaged*, are importantly and distinctly different!

Not too long ago, most of the educational literature used those two terms interchangeably. The literature seemed to imply that if a student was on task, he was automatically and naturally engaged. The more time that goes by, the more differently these two ideas have been treated. Thankfully, the literature is beginning to change, and writers and researchers are starting to delineate the difference between the two.

One of the easiest ways to illustrate this difference is with an actual illustration. Consider On-Task in Figure 3.1. He looks happy enough, he is awake, he is alert, and it is probably safe to assume that he even sits still in his chair. The information is going in, and he can spit it right back out for the test. No matter that when he does regurgitate the information, it remains unchanged from the way it went in. But what about Engaged in Figure 3.2? The information is in there, too, but he is *doing something* with it. It is rolling around in there (processing), the gears are turning (cognition), and he is making meaning for himself (constructivism). This is obviously nothing like what is happening with On-Task.

These pictures represent the stark difference between two very important ideas, and they contain a simple message for those who teach. Too often teachers are happy to have On-Task in class. He is quiet and listening, and when the principal walks in, she will note that he is on task. Unfortunately, some teachers even prefer On-Task; after all, he makes very few demands of the teacher.

The really model student, however, the one schools really need to cultivate, is Engaged. He may not be quiet, but he is listening and thinking, and if the teacher is lucky, he will ask questions. *Real* questions! Not, "How do you spell that?" The really good questions, ones like, "Why does that happen?" "Why would they do that?" "What happens if . . . ?" The teacher may be teaching On-Task, but Engaged is learning!

Even though Engaged is the student whom teachers should want, sometimes the system shuts him down. The biggest problem with Engaged is that he likes to be engaged. If the instruction gets too boring, he is likely to create his own excitement, which is often termed Disruptive.

To clarify the difference between On-Task and Engaged, it may be instructive to go to an expert. Actual students are probably the most underuti-

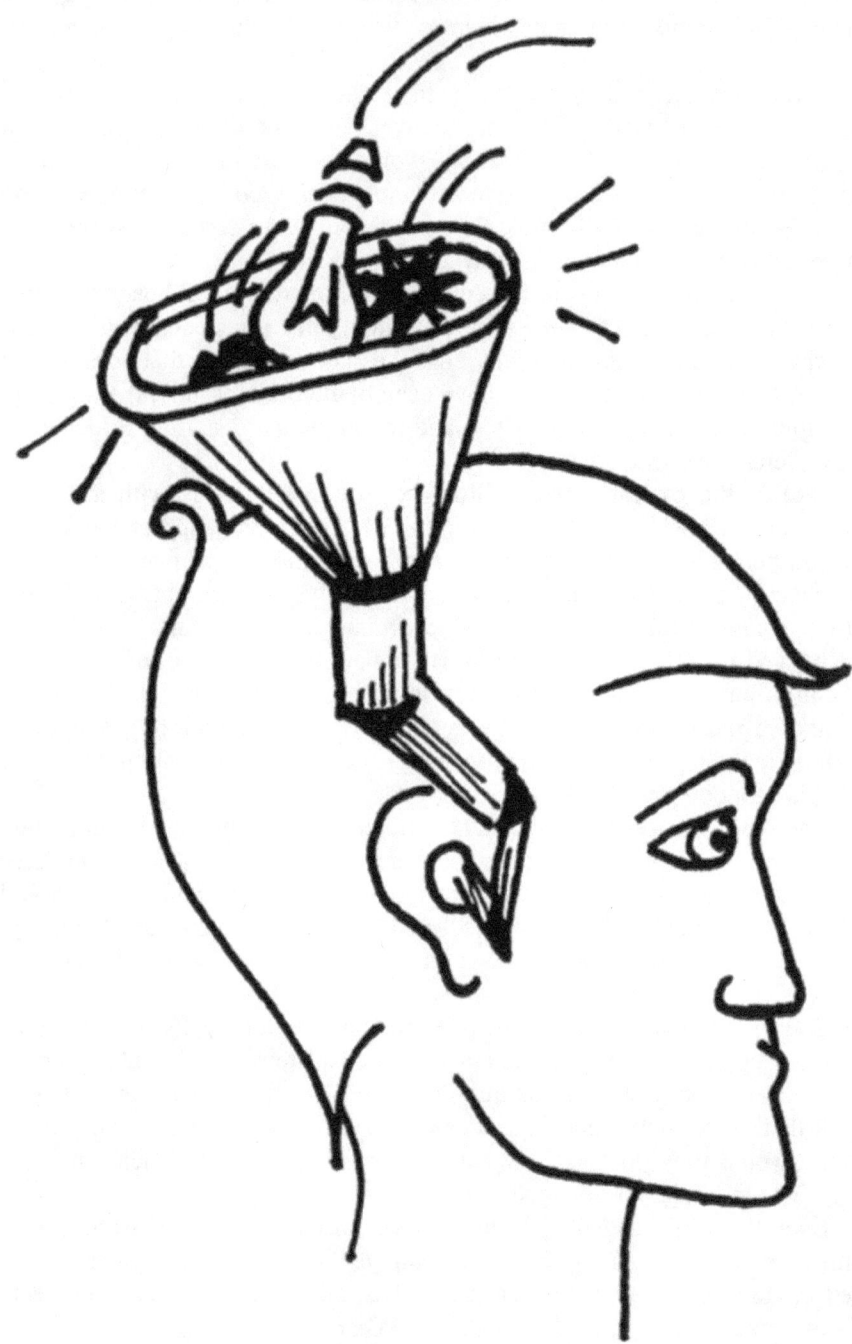

Figure 3.1. "On-Task." Emily Woll.

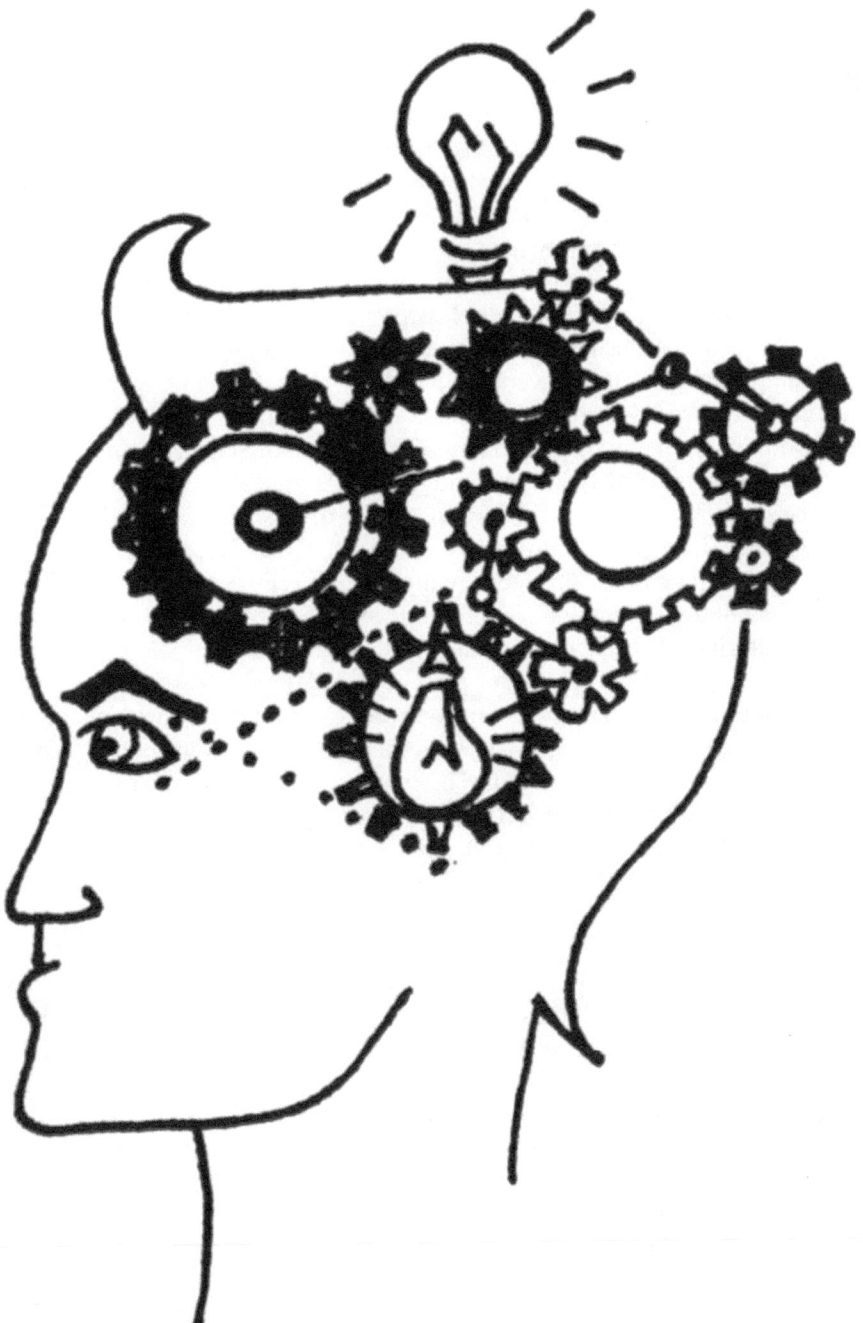

Figure 3.2. "Engaged." Emily Woll.

lized professional development experts in the world. After all, they observe teachers all day, and not just for quick drop-ins, either. They see a wide variety of teaching styles and strategies, and at the secondary level they see these across different content areas.

Conversations with middle school students can be particularly interesting. They spend more time in actual classrooms than any administrator, and most kids in that age bracket are happy to share exactly what they really think, not just what the adult wants to hear. It may not be politically correct, or even kind, but it is usually brutally honest.

Explain the difference between on-task and engaged, show the pictures, and ask these kids how often their classrooms are truly engaging, and middle schoolers, without hesitation, often respond, "Oh, almost never." Then ask another question: "What if every day, in every class, for just five minutes the classroom was really engaging?" Watch what happens as they visualize what that would look like in their own lives. They light up. School could be a very different place for students. Even with just five minutes' difference.

The cold, hard truth about way too much of what happens in the classroom is that it is boring. Educators hate to use that word, but there it is, *boring*. Sometimes class can just be boring for a little while, but way too often it is mind-numbingly boring for long stretches. No teacher will admit to being that kind of teacher, but strangely enough, everyone knows someone who is.

Anyone with a school-aged child—a son, daughter, niece, nephew, grandchild, or neighbor—has heard and seen this complaint about school. What a tragedy! If just five minutes a day in every class, every day was engaging, students' lives would be very different. It is easy to make the argument that if schools could achieve this for five minutes, every day, in every class, the students would not let it stop there. They would push their teachers to create an environment that was more often engaging and less often boring.

In one of the biggest ironies of schools, it can be the "at risk" student who is often the canary in the mineshaft. "At risk" students are like the story, "The Emperor's New Clothes." This is an old story that tells of a pompous and vain emperor who hires two charlatans when they promise to provide him with magic clothes. Their cloth, they claim, can only be seen by the wise; to the foolish it is invisible.

When the emperor sends the wisest men in the kingdom to check on the progress of the two villains, they are quick to return and report great progress. Of course they don't want to admit to being fools who cannot see the cloth. When the emperor dons his new and magical "clothes," he, too, is silent, not wanting to reveal his own foolishness.

It is only as the emperor leads a parade dressed only in his undergarments that a small child in the crowd shouts out that the emperor has no clothes. At this point, the ingenious hucksters are discovered. Naturally they are already safely out of town.

In schools, it seems that the "at risk" student is the small child of the story, and the teachers and administrators are the emperor and the wise men of the kingdom. The adults strut around in their wisdom, continuing the same practices whether or not they are successful. How often is it that the student no one really wants in class in the first place is the first one to voice what the others are thinking? *"This is boring."*

It is naïve to believe that every moment of the school day can be thrilling and exciting and highly engaging; that would be exhausting both for teachers and for students. Just for a moment though, let your mind wander. What if the world of school was more often engaging and less often boring? The world of education could be a much different place, and just maybe it can be done for not much more effort than is already expended trying to suck the life out of things that are inherently interesting.

Sounds intriguing, but how can teachers move from the world of "on task" to the world of "engaged"? The answer brings the conversation back around to an earlier topic. If schools and teachers focused more on the learning than on the teaching, if teachers really internalized the difference and made student learning the real target, what would that look like in schools?

If the approach to every lesson begins by looking at the curriculum guide—not the district or state guide, but the teacher outline that was created in the last chapter—then the starting point would be: *What do I want my students to know, and why do I want them to know it?* Most importantly, teachers would genuinely be able to answer the question, *What can I ask students to do that will cause them to know what I want them to know?* The answer to this question will have teaching headed in the direction of learning.

Time for concrete examples. Start with the boring model: Read the chapter, answer the questions at the end of the chapter, take the test created by the textbook publisher. Even for schools that have long ago rejected this model, most educators can still name someone who uses it regularly, if not exclusively.

So what to do instead? Start with the chapter in the textbook. What is in the chapter that the curriculum says that students should know? If the book does a really good job at explaining a concept, by all means use it; just don't think that by simply reading the words, the knowledge will be absorbed and internalized by students. If it was that easy, then the textbook could just be sent home with the students and school districts could save on the heating bills.

Instead of just reading the words, what can students do to *engage* with the words? What task will interest them enough that they will look like Engaged? A simple strategy is to have them illustrate the words. Think about it: It is not possible to draw a picture of something that is not understood. What would you draw? A student has to have at least a rudimentary grasp of a concept in order to render any kind of illustration.

As an added bonus, a quick glance at a student-created picture can tell a teacher instantly if the student understands the material in the correct context or not. No need for ponderous formative assessments to determine whether or not the student understands the concept.

Want to use words? Have the students write a letter using the text as a starting point. They could write an explanation to a younger student, or write what they think should happen in the next chapter, or write questions about the material—the list is as long as the imagination.

Struggling with higher-level questions? Give students that list of stem words that was handed out at that in-service last year. The one teachers use to write those official curriculum documents. Everyone has seen it, the one with the DOK (Depth of Knowledge) words on it; this used to be called "Bloom's Taxonomy," remember? Have students write two questions from each DOK level, making sure they can answer the questions they have created. Want to get them moving? Make the lesson kinesthetic. Have them write the question on a piece of paper and then have a paper ball fight; everyone grabs a ball and has to answer the question.

What if the book does a terrible job or is so boring or densely written that it would cure insomnia? Just read a short passage, then give students the information in notes, from a short film clip, or on PowerPoint, etc. The point is that the most important step is to first identify exactly what the student should know and why he should know it, then from there develop the strategy used to teach the material becomes much less formidable.

The bottom line is that the process of designing lesson plans should not start with the activity but rather with the objective. Once the teacher can clearly articulate what a student should know and why they should know it, developing a task that allows the student to learn and then demonstrate his knowledge becomes much less overwhelming.

New instructional strategies seem to be the resource that teachers request most frequently. Countless professional development opportunities are offered to increase teachers' tool kits. There are more examples of interesting educational activities than any one book could contain. These resources are readily available to most teachers, and thousands more examples exist on the Internet. If this is the case, however, why do teachers consistently ask for more concrete examples? Maybe sometimes teachers just don't know what to ask for.

This is not as silly as it sounds, and it is certainly not a criticism of teachers. Teachers really are amazing problem-solvers. It is more often than not the case that when teachers can articulate a specific problem, they can quickly develop countless creative solutions to the problem. One of the biggest blocks to engaged classrooms is not a lack of strategies, but rather a lack of focus on the end game.

Most teachers don't need more examples of activities, even though this is what teachers often ask for. What is needed are more reminders to stop and think about the goal. The question teachers need to ask themselves when planning instruction is, *What am I trying to teach, and why am I teaching it in the first place?* This is where the different components of teaching start to work together.

The answer to these questions was already identified in the guide that was the focus of the previous chapter. Using the curriculum guide to plan instruction, to plan for the actual learning, keeps the focus on what students need to know.

Once there is a clear picture of the goal, student mastery of the objectives, figuring out how to set the students up to actually learn the material becomes much easier. When the goal moves to understanding key concepts and moves away from the repetition of a set of facts, engaging activities become much more obvious.

This may be why so many of the books on the market seem unsatisfying to classroom teachers. Most schools have a plethora of books with countless examples of engaging lessons. Yet teachers almost universally complain about a lack of concrete examples. What teachers may really be asking for is not examples but rationale. If the "what" to teach (curriculum) has a clear purpose, then the "how" to teach (instruction) flows out much more naturally.

It is easy to become distracted by the latest fad in instructional strategies. Too often the activity drives the lesson instead of the learning objective driving the lesson. Using the curriculum guide, with the objective clearly delineated, keeps the focus on the learning instead of the teaching.

Brain research indicates that the brain likes novelty. Even a short time spent in and around schools will show this to be the case. Students love to do new things; conversely, even the coolest project or activity loses its power to engage if it becomes too familiar. When designing lessons, get in the habit of asking a couple of basic questions: *What do I want them to know? How can I get them to understand it? What can we do to practice this new idea so they will remember it, really learn it?*

As seems to be so often the case, these ideas are not new, nor are they revolutionary (and they don't need new names to be useful!). This thinking through of the goal and objectives is the kind of thinking work that needs to happen before planning actual lessons. Almost every teacher does this at the beginning of the year. What doesn't always happen is an ongoing review of the curriculum guide when planning individual units throughout the year.

See if this scenario sounds familiar. The teacher starts the year off with all sorts of good intentions; the first unit is fabulous. There are interesting and meaningful projects, things are organized, life is good. Then comes October, parent-teacher conferences are coming, grades are due, students have settled in, classroom management takes more time, grading is becoming a chore . . . The honeymoon is way over.

What happens? Sadly, what often happens is that the teacher goes back to the old, familiar strategies. Students read from the text, the teacher lectures, the students take notes, then out come the worksheets. This progression doesn't happen because these strategies have suddenly become engaging. Teachers use these tired old strategies to help them to keep their own sanity and, even more sadly, to keep the students quiet. How, then, can teachers avoid falling into this trap?

Two things can be useful to get over this hump. One, put into place some visual reminders to keep asking the questions that should be asked. (A Post-it Note that gets moved to the end of each section as planning happens works great.) Two, make a personal pledge not to use any "activity" more than twice a year. This keeps the thinking happening throughout the school year and helps to keep the focus on new ways to interact with the material.

These examples work for any content area and probably for any grade level, and they go on and on. It doesn't take teachers long to come up with fabulous ideas for engaging activities. Even teachers who are viewed as mediocre can come up with really cool strategies if they are asked the right questions.

Keep this in mind: The brain likes novelty! Even the most exciting activity gets old if repeated too often. Not all ideas work as well as others, so it is important to just keep it moving. Activities that don't go as planned, or even fail, are usually not as deadly as the questions at the end of the chapter in the textbook. A failed activity can even be a great learning opportunity. Get the students to help design a better way to run an activity. Have them debrief and help to determine why the lesson failed.

Remember: It is the learning that is more important than the act of teaching. If, at the end of the day, the students have grown in their understanding of a concept that is important for them to grasp, learning has happened. Mission accomplished!

It is not at all uncommon to hear teachers lament that some content areas are naturally more interesting than others and that is the reason that some teachers seem more engaging to the students. In other words, it's easy to be engaging if the material is engaging. This sounds logical, but listen to how kids talk about school. Almost universally, when students are asked about their favorite subject, they will name their favorite teacher.

One year kids like Science; the next year they love Math or Communication Arts. Listen, and there will be the same refrain from almost all of them: "Mr. Jones's class is so cool, *I love the way he teaches.*" Hear that? It's not the content, but *the way the content is presented*. In teacher speak, the strategies the teacher uses are what makes the classroom engaging (or boring).

In order to increase student achievement, schools have to create a climate that is more engaging. It is as simple as that. The way to make it engaging is by using all those cool teaching strategies. Every teacher knows the strategies; they can all list the projects. The trick is to always keep in mind the goal; to coin a phrase, "Keep the main thing, the main thing."

And once again the conversation circles back. Without a clear picture of what students should learn, which is the curriculum, teachers become caught in the familiar trap: doing the same old, same old (boring). The question becomes, how to keep the teachers on the right track? When curriculum and planning work hand in hand with instruction, interesting lessons are the natural outflow.

Know what the main thing is: what the students need to know. Then follow up with the answer to the question, How will they learn it? Once the "main thing" is the main thing, teachers, schools, and ultimately students will be headed in the right direction and away from the enemy of learning—boredom.

KEY IDEAS TO REMEMBER

- Teaching and learning are not necessarily the same thing. No matter how inspired the teaching, if students are not learning, classrooms are not effective.
- Student engagement is the key to learning. Without engagement, school often becomes "boring."
- Curriculum should drive instruction. Use the curriculum guide to keep the focus on the objectives.
- Instructional activities are the means to an end, not an end in themselves.
- Keep the main thing, the main thing. What do students need to know? How will they learn it?

QUESTIONS FOR FURTHER REFLECTION

- How would you describe the difference between teaching and learning in your own classroom/school?
- Poll your students to get an idea of their views of the amount of time that is engaging versus on task in your classroom/school. Poll the staff and ask the same question. Do the two match? Discuss the reasons for the responses you receive.

- How many different instructional strategies do you use in a unit of study? In a semester? How could you increase the time students are engaged versus on task in your classroom/school?

Chapter Four

Grades That Tell the Whole Story

Grading is so intricately tied to instruction that this could easily be a part of the last chapter. While instruction is one of the most important aspects of teaching, the one that is most likely to arouse passions is grading. Grading and grading practices are the areas that seem to cause the most grief to teachers and students alike. The majority of teachers would share that they have had little to no real formal training in how, or even why, to grade. It is no surprise then that teachers often feel at a loss in dealing with grading.

To start at the beginning, why assess grades? Two obvious reasons are to give students feedback on their learning and to provide parents with information about how their child is progressing. Consider all the other things grading is used for, however: student ranking, teacher proficiency, college entrance, student motivation, classroom rigor, scholarship eligibility, insurance discounts . . . the longer the list, the more complicated it becomes.

How can something that has so much weight, both inside school and in the larger world, have so little training attached to it? How can teachers unravel grading and make it work for and not against both students and teachers?

One thing at a time. First, why should teachers give students feedback? The answer is fairly obvious. How can anyone know if they are on the right track, if they are "getting it," unless they have some feedback on their progress? Feedback is critical to learning; this is intrinsically true. Anyone who has been around small children can see the basic human need for feedback.

A baby stands on her own for the first time and looks to the adults in the room for confirmation that standing is good. A toddler gets the food from the bowl, to the mouth, on the spoon, and looks for approval that this is the way eating is done. A preschool child ties his shoe unaided and looks up to get feedback. As humans, there is a built-in need for feedback, preferably positive feedback, as a guide to learning.

Teachers and parents often lament the fact that young people would rather play video games than do anything connected with school. While video games hold this kind of appeal for many reasons, one of the biggest reasons is because they usually provide instant and definitive feedback.

Think about it: You push the button and see the reaction; you either get further in the game and go to the next level, or you make a mistake, the game ends and play begins again. This feedback loop—the short and immediate feedback loop—is a big part of what makes the game interesting.

How many young people would continue to play these games, even the gory, inappropriate ones, if pushing the buttons didn't result in immediate action? Would the game be fun if the players had to go through the whole level before they found out whether or not they were successful? As frustrating as failure is, it is one of the most necessary features of the game.

If even something as overtly appealing as video games relies on feedback to maintain interest, how much more do schools and teachers need to make sure that they are giving feedback to students? This feedback needs to be timely (not weeks after the event), and it needs to be chunked, that is, not only present at the very end.

A teacher tells a student that the project he has worked on for more than thirty minutes is wrong and that he, the student, needs to begin again. Anyone who has ever been in a classroom can predict the reaction, can't they? First the student looks at the adult in disbelief; maybe he argues that what he has done really is what was asked for. Then, more likely than not, the student puts his head down or otherwise withdraws from the assignment. Severe reactions can escalate to full-out rebellion, complete with a trip to the office.

Remember the video game. It doesn't allow the players to play incorrectly for too long before they "die." Players see their progress right there on the screen. Even more importantly, if the player is going down in flames, they don't have to wait long to start again; they "die" quickly and then immediately get to start over. Certainly no one is suggesting that students "die" in class, but the longer students go before they are required to start incorrect work over, the more frustration there will be when they do have to go back.

Too many times, school just doesn't work like that. A student can sometimes be required to completely finish a lengthy assignment, only to find out later that it was completed incorrectly. Even worse, many times students do not even receive feedback in the form of a grade until weeks after the project is completed. Not only is the feedback received after the learning is over, but it is received with no follow-up opportunity to complete the task correctly. How does this impact the ultimate goal of learning?

Young people are more clever than they are sometimes given credit for. How many times is a young person in a classroom given the clear message that the grade is completely disassociated from learning the material? The grade then becomes the thing to be sought after and not the learning. How sad that those two things become either/or choices.

On the surface, it seems logical that grades should be a positive motivator for students. Consider the actual motivational value of grades. When the message from the teacher is that the learning is not the goal, that is a completely abstract concept; if a letter on a piece of paper is the goal, how motivating is that to a concrete learner?

Students need feedback, but so do their parents. The first questions most parents have involve grades. Parents want to know if little Johnny is being successful. Many educators are also parents and they can relate. Adults want to know grades for two reasons: so they can be proud of their own little Johnny when he masters the material, and so that he can get assistance, if he needs it, as soon as possible. More on the outside-the-classroom ramifications of grading in the next chapter.

Grading can be hard. No educator wants children to sit and endure the feeling of defeat they will feel when they are not successful, and neither do their parents. Everyone wants grading to be able to yield the information that is needed to help students, but do grades really provide that information?

Teachers use grades not just as feedback, but also to motivate students. Whether anyone really believes this motivates them or not, grades are used as the hammer that hangs over their heads. "You want to get a good grade, so you need to . . ." "You will fail the test if you don't . . ." It may very well be this dubious use of grades that causes most of the problems that teachers and schools get themselves into with parents.

The tragedy is that for all of their use as a negative consequence, it is entirely possible that the rest of the world generally doesn't share the same view of grades as do teachers. What seems to professional educators as the worst possible fate may not be similarly viewed by their students.

Grades are important to those who spend their careers inside schools. Educators have spent all, or at the very least a large part, of their lives being successful in schools. They were usually the good students; otherwise they would not have chosen to spend their waking hours in schools as adults.

Even those teachers who as students struggled in school until they met that one teacher who helped them to be successful, were, in the end, successful. What kind of person would willingly go into a field that took them back to the very place where they were the most miserable? Face it, even those teachers who didn't think of themselves as the "smart kid" found some level of success and comfort in school or they would not have gone back into the classroom in the first place.

Teachers are the ones who, as students, cared about their grades, and they often quite frankly find it difficult to understand that there are large parts of the population who do not. Grades motivate teachers, and the threat of a bad grade will goad teachers into doing things that they don't really want to do. These highly educated individuals who have made education their life's work are still in thrall to grades.

For anyone who doubts the power of grades on teachers, observe the effect of any new teacher evaluation instrument. No matter how the evaluations are set up, teachers will translate the categories into letter grades. Everyone knows that the highest category on any assessment is equivalent to an A.

Try as they may, administrators will attempt to explain that the "Exceeds Expectation" category is *over and above* the level that is required, and that not all teachers will be able to meet this level. Exceeds Expectation, administrators insist, is not an A. But listen in the teachers' lounge, and it will be clear that teachers who do not meet that level are hurt. Many teachers were the A students in school and still really want the top grade. Teachers are the products of schools, and schools are all about grades.

That all students do not hold grades in the same high regard should not be a surprise, it may be maddening, but it should not be surprising. If this is known to be true, then why use grades as a motivator? If only there was a good answer to this question. It is probably the case that many times teachers use grades this way subconsciously. What is clear is the underlying assumption in most schools that students will perform for the grade.

Just listen when teachers explain assignments, return graded work, or talk to parents about class grades. Unspoken is the absolute belief that a good grade is a motivator to students to continue to excel. The converse is just as absolute: A bad grade will cause a student to try harder the next time.

It doesn't take a lot of convincing to make teachers aware, at an intellectual level, that not all students are motivated by grades. However, even though they know it won't work, teachers go back down that road time and again. They threaten the F if the work is not done properly or is not turned in on time. Perhaps the reason for this is that too often educators "do school" the way school is "done."

Educational professionals are creatures of the environment that birthed them. School is about doing work, getting grades, taking tests, and moving on. No one intends to perpetuate the ineffectiveness of the past, but it is so insidiously easy to get caught up in the model, unless something deliberate happens to break us out of the mold.

Follow the traditional line of reasoning. Students are given work to do in the hope that the completion of that work will help them to learn and understand the concepts that are being taught. Teachers want students to do the work, because if they do, they will learn: Mission accomplished! When students meet the expectations, the model works and is thereby perpetuated.

The problem comes when students don't do the work. They are then given poor grades so that they will be motivated to do the work in the future to avoid failure. But what about the student who simply does not want to do the work? If the student does not particularly care about the grade, he would rather have a poor grade (which does not matter to him anyway) instead of doing something he doesn't want to do.

Picture the kid who doesn't want to do the work. Would she rather write the essay or get an F? All too often, the lesser of the two evils, from the student's point of view, is the poor grade. As a result, the student will not do the work, she fails to master the material, she then fails the class, and the teacher is left to explain to parents and/or administrators why the student is failing. Then, if this happens at the high school level, the student has to take the class again. What a recipe for disaster!

Continue just a little deeper into the storyline. The student does not do the homework and the teacher issues a disciplinary consequence to the student. When this particular story reaches its climax, the teacher is angry because the work was not done, the student is angry because now they have been disciplined, which makes school seem even more unpleasant, and the parent is angry because the student has failed.

Add to this the work on brain research that reveals that the frontal lobe, in charge of executive functioning, is not completely developed until a young person is in their early twenties. This part of the brain is responsible for linking cause and effect. In essence, the average young person is not developmentally capable of independently making good decisions, especially those decisions that involve an unpleasant task in the short term for a reward in the long term.

Brace for the next scenario; it gets even messier. A student, the difficult one, the smart kid who does not do the work, this student gets a whole row of zeroes in the grade book and then somehow passes the test. Another student, the polite one who tries really hard but is not great at tests, does all the work, gets lots of good scores on homework, but fails the test, probably not by a huge margin, but they still fail. What is a teacher to do?

It turns out that most teachers will willingly fudge the books to assign a passing grade to the polite student, the one who did not master the material. This means that the student who does not master the content goes to the next level without having really learned that material.

The same teacher is angry with the student who passed the test but didn't do the homework. Even with passing test grades, the missing homework grades will be reflected, and so the student who did understand the material has so many zeroes on homework that they fail. This student will be required to sit through the class again?

How can this be a good idea? What are teachers thinking? The student who acquired the knowledge is required to learn material they already know. The student who did not acquire the knowledge is allowed to go to the next level without the requisite foundation. Usually there is not any thinking about it at all. Teachers look at the row of grades in the grade book. The chips fall where they may. Numbers are objective.

The student with missing assignments does not have the required number of points to move to the next level, and so they fail; they brought it on themselves. The student was warned that this would happen if they did not do the assignments and so the teacher doesn't feel bad at all. The polite student is a hard worker, nice, and polite, and anyone can justify making small adjustments because that nice, hardworking student doesn't deserve to fail. What a mess!

So, what does a grade mean? Some teachers are going to be unhappy with this next statement, and disagree vehemently, but the fact is that very often the grade means absolutely nothing. Nothing? How can that be? All that work—grading papers, pestering kids to get work turned in—and it means nothing? Teachers are professionals, grades do matter, how can they mean nothing?

At one conference led by Dr. Robert Marzano, he began with an interesting activity, something like this. He asked those in the room to imagine that they, as teachers, had given a test. Ten of the questions were lower-level questions, ten were higher-level questions but the material was explicitly taught, and ten questions were higher-level questions and the material was not explicitly taught. He then asked the teachers to assign point values to the levels of questions.

Next he asked the teachers to imagine that a student had answered all of the lower-level questions correctly, half of the higher-level/explicitly taught items correctly, but had answered none of the higher-level/not explicitly taught items correctly. Then came the moment of truth: What was the student's grade?

It turns out that in a room of several hundred educators, the student received anywhere from an A to an F on *the same assessment,* and that is with no regard whatsoever to the actual questions! Add in the differences in the way that teachers weigh homework, and it is easy to see that grades are not the objective numbers in the grade book that teachers like to think they are. This also calls into question assessment practices, but more on that in the next chapter.

What is a teacher to do?

Go back to the drawing board. Why do schools want to grade students anyway? That's not so hard: Schools want students to understand the progress they are making and they want others (parents, administrators, etc.) to know the same thing. Okay, that seems logical enough; now back up one more step and ask, progress toward what?

It is at this point that one of the main objectives of this book becomes clear. None of the different parts of teaching happens in a vacuum; they are all connected. Back in Chapter 2, there was a discussion about what to teach.

Follow the logical progression: If teachers want to know whether or not students are learning, it is necessary to go back and remember what it was that the teacher thought that the student should know in the first place.

Look at the grades that are tracked in the grade book. Do they accurately reflect a student's mastery of the things that the teacher wanted them to know? It is very easy to get so tied up in the everyday process of managing groups of students that we lose track of the goal. There is a reason that the metaphor "can't see the forest for the trees" was coined.

Of all the places that teaching can change, no change may be as profound as the way that teachers need to change in relationship to the tracking of grades.

When starting out as a beginning teacher, we usually understand that the job of the teacher is to assign work to students, collect the work, grade it, and then enter all those numbers into the grade book. At the end of each grading period, teachers then report on the student's grade, believing that it is an accurate reflection of student learning; after all, numbers don't lie.

This is the way that almost all of the classes teachers have ever taken calculated grades. It is the way most cooperating teachers did it when today's teachers were student teaching. This is how school works. It is very difficult to see beyond the way things are done and to think that there might be another way, much less a better way.

What if grading was really based on the knowledge that the student had acquired? Could grades be based on learning, not on teaching?

Here is one way to explain what grading can look like, and it makes a great way to explain it to students and their parents: If a person were on the basketball team (groan . . . not a sports analogy!) and they were doing drills, would anyone keep score? Of course not. The purpose of drills is to learn the skills, to get better; the appropriate time to keep score is when the game is played.

So why can't that same thinking be used in a classroom? The drills (the assignments) are done so that the student can learn the skill. Keeping score (grading) while doing the learning doesn't make sense. Why would anyone want to put a score on their attempts at learning when they are still learning? It still makes sense to keep track of the learning, to see that progress is being made, but making an assessment of what students know is something that should happen at the end, not while the learning is still going on.

After all, if Student #1 learns the material at a high level, he gets an A. What if Student #2 did not learn the material as quickly? What if on some of the formative assessments the student received a low mark? Does that second student's learning not equal the first student's learning when the summative is complete? In a traditional gradebook, where all the points are added up and averaged, the second student did not learn as much as the first.

What could that look like in an engaged classroom? Students still do lots of work, but almost no worksheets and never the questions at the end of the chapter; instead students complete lots of projects. They may do illustrated timelines, storyboards, mini-books, board games, posters, stations, anything that students will find engaging. The goal is to give the students a chance to play with the material as a means to learning.

Most teachers do at least some of these kind of projects. The difference, in a classroom that is centered on learning, is this: Don't just grade this work and record it in the gradebook. Do give students feedback, just not a recorded grade for classwork. Realize that students are just as excited by a checkmark as they are by a letter grade. Give them a √+ and they understand this is equal to an A. They will also understand that a √– is unacceptable.

The point is that it is possible to give students feedback about their learning without giving final judgment of what they have learned. After all, the project or classwork is about the process of learning. Students are doing the work to acquire the knowledge, not to demonstrate their mastery of it.

Well, says the stickler down the hall, if students don't get grades for the work they do, why would they bother to do it? To begin with, classwork must be designed to be engaging on its own. If students want to do the work because the work itself is engaging, they will learn more from that work.

Sometimes finishing an assignment is not as important as working on it. Oh gosh, was that just in print? Well, yes, if students are labeling a map, is it more important that they learn to transfer information from the book to their paper, identify the important information, and learn where things are? Or is the goal of the assignment just to finish the assignment? Sometimes finishing is important; sometimes just playing with the information is the goal. The point is that the goal of the assignment needs to drive the way that the assignment is assessed.

Another example: A teacher has students use their vocabulary words to create a crossword puzzle. Very often, in classrooms, crosswords puzzles are a waste of time. Having students merely write the word in a blank is hardly a way to develop their understanding of the word. However, having students develop the clues for a puzzle is a whole other proposition. Clues are different from definitions.

Definitions, as every student knows, are just an exercise in copying sentences from the glossary; it is not even necessary to actually know what any of the words mean to be able to successfully complete the task. Creating clues from the definition requires that the student *understand* the word, much more in line with the goal of learning.

After creating the clues, the students put the words into a grid; in effect they create the key to the puzzle, and only then could they create a blank puzzle. Observe: The actual learning involved is at the very beginning of the project, when they create the clue. Creating the actual puzzle is just the fun part. It doesn't really matter if they finish the "assignment" (creating the puzzle); what matters is whether or not they have an understanding of the vocabulary.

In a little bit of teacher trickery, this teacher gave those who used their time wisely and finished creating a puzzle the chance to trade puzzles with each other; those who did not use their time wisely were given a much less attractive alternative. This was a much more meaningful consequence to students for an incomplete assignment than a poor grade.

What has traditionally happened in schools is that grades are used to motivate students to do the work. Remember the discussion at the beginning of this chapter? The problem is that the students who need the most motivation are the very ones who are not motivated by grades at all.

Another story to illustrate the point. John was not motivated by grades; his first priority was always to get the work moved from his in-box to the teacher's in-box. Since he was not motivated by grades, he did not care if he received a poor grade, and consequently he rushed through, or more often did not turn in, his assignments. The teacher recorded the failing grades just as he deserved.

The problem was that the teacher really wanted John to learn the material, which he did not. The teacher viewed the F as a negative consequence for John. John, on the other hand, got what he wanted—to avoid doing the work. Who was served by this approach? Clearly, no one. John got what he wanted, which was not to do the work, but was he well served? Not if the goal was to have him "know and be able to do. . . ." The teacher was left frustrated because the consequences were not changing the behavior, which was certainly the goal for the teacher.

Here is another approach. If the teacher determines that the completion of a particular assignment is necessary for the student to learn the material at the level that is intended, then the completion of the assignment is not negotiable. Do not allow students to decide to take a "0" and not do the work. If the work is not completed in the time allotted, require the student to come during lunch or stay after school until it is finished.

This is much more of a negative consequence than a bad grade. It is not a stretch of the imagination to see that students who may not be motivated by grades care much more about "their" time than they do about their grades. The negative consequences need to actually be negative to the recipient if they are to motivate a change in behavior.

Grades seem like such a simple concept. They have been an integral part of schools from time immemorial, and yet when the layers are peeled back, they are not simple at all. Grades have many functions, some of which will be further discussed in the following chapter. One of the key functions of grades is to provide students, parents, and others with feedback regarding students' educational progress.

But since grades have been part of the landscape for such a long time, they now come with lots of extra baggage. Simply providing feedback is hardly the only use that teachers make of student grades, but perhaps it is time to reevaluate.

So often in education, the traps that bog teachers down are rooted in practices that have become messy and diluted with years of added layers of meaning. It is time to peel back those layers and reestablish student grades as a legitimate and meaningful means of providing feedback to students that genuinely reflects what they have actually learned.

And so another chapter closes, but the refrain remains the same. The components of teaching that began in Chapter 2 with curriculum and carried on through instruction in Chapter 3 are part of what informs the practice of grading.

In addition to the interconnectedness of curriculum, instruction, and grading, the bigger lesson in this chapter deals with the theory behind the work. When teachers stop and consider the theory behind the purpose of grading, it naturally changes how they calculate student grades. Grading is perhaps one of the least addressed areas in teacher professional development. Now is the time to reexamine.

Taking a fresh look at grading practices, in light of the course objectives that were established in Chapter 2, is critical if grades are to mean what they are purported to mean. Using grades as a stick to coerce students into completing work against their will is not only ineffective, it is bad practice.

Giving students feedback about their learning is one of the most important things that teachers do. Traditionally, teachers have looked at feedback just as the grade that the student receives. Grades are certainly a piece of the puzzle, but they don't have to be the only piece. For feedback to work, it needs to be real for students; it needs to be a part of the instruction and not just a letter or number on a page at the end of the unit.

As the synergy between the various components of teaching grows, using curriculum to very clearly lay out exactly *what a student needs to know* combines with grades that equally clearly show *what a student has learned*. The power that is generated by the thoughtful interaction of these two teacher tasks creates a more effective classroom with better outcomes for both student and teacher.

KEY IDEAS TO REMEMBER

- Feedback is critical to student learning.
- Accurate and timely feedback is absolutely necessary if students are to persevere in their learning.

- Using grades as an incentive for student effort is largely ineffective, especially with difficult students.
- Grades should represent accurate and timely feedback of student progress toward mastery of the objectives that are clearly delineated in the curriculum.
- Determining a student's level of mastery by totaling points earned during the learning process instead of assessing the mastery of the course objectives leads to grades that do not provide accurate information to students or parents.

QUESTIONS FOR FURTHER REFLECTION

- How often and in what ways do you give your students feedback about their progress toward mastery?
- What are the components of a student's grade in your classroom/school?
- Compare your students' test grades to their final course grades. Do they match? What do students and their parents know about student mastery of curricular goals?

Chapter Five

Grading with Meaning

Now on to the other major function of grading: giving parents and others outside the school setting information about a student's progress. When looking at the grade for a specific student in any given class, can anyone be confident that the grade is indeed an accurate description of that student's ability? What about comparing grades between different classes? Do grades really give the information they purport to give?

Grades are used for lots of reasons, student placement being one of them. Are the grades that students receive more about what the student has learned, or are they more about the amount of work that a student has done? Are the students who are placed in a specific academic setting based on past grades, in the right setting after all?

Most school systems use traditional A, B, C, D, F, or 4-point scales, and since they are so familiar, these labels are thrown around with a confidence that seems so certain. What does this mean? Think about any discussion of student progress, including conversations with other teachers, with parents, or with administrators in meetings about students. Hear a teacher say with great certainty, "He has an A in class, so that means he has really learned the material," "She is at a C, so she needs to study harder," or "He failed, he didn't learn a thing." But for all the certainty, what does that grade really mean?

Every teacher believes that they know what specific grades mean in their classrooms, but what about the previous year's teacher, and what will this year's grade mean to the next teacher? In what may come as a surprise to those outside the field of education, there really is no set standard. It seems as if there is a commonly agreed-upon criteria and most educators act as if there is indeed such a standard. However, it doesn't take much reflection to realize that any criteria that does exist is illusory at best.

What is more, schools act as if everyone in the larger world also knows what that standard is based on. Just listen to non-educators talk about the experience of their own children, and it quickly becomes clear that the standards upon which so many decisions are based are loosely defined, if they are defined at all.

This turns into quicksand very fast, and the longer one thinks about it, the messier it gets. How can grades be used as a standard comparison when there is no standard, when in effect every teacher sets his own standard? That would be like declaring that all currency worldwide is completely interchangeable. If there is no set standard, what is a grade really worth?

The good news is that most people, in and out of educational circles, can give a pretty clear explanation of what each grade should represent. An A means the student really gets it, they understand the material at the level of instruction; a B means they are almost there.

On the other hand, a C means they have some gaps, they get pieces but they are not solid on all the material; a D means they are not really there at all, they have big gaps and are in danger of not really understanding; and an F means they do not understand, they did not learn what was expected.

These definitions work fairly well in the abstract when discussing a particular piece of work, but what happens when work is averaged together? What does a grade mean when it includes homework, classwork, and participation points? What seems simple becomes more complicated by the minute.

It would be safe to wager that most people would agree that the definitions, as described above, are at least in the ballpark. If, however, a group of teachers was brought together, they could pick those definitions to pieces in short order. See the point about the quicksand above. Notwithstanding the complications, this is the system that is in place, however, and so teachers have to make do with the tools at hand.

Using the descriptors for grades given above, go back to the question, do the grades students earn reflect their true mastery (or lack thereof) of the material that was taught? All too often they do not. Beyond the confusion caused by loose criteria, for many classrooms, grades are a hodgepodge of lots of different kinds of information. How can this be?

It seems that grades are one of the only things many teachers feel that they really still have control over. For that reason, grades too often become both the carrot and the stick that teachers use to control the chaos. Teachers use grades to reward and to punish. And if that was not confusing enough, sometimes grades are weighted or even curved.

Seasoned teachers remember well the days when the bell curve was the model. The underlying belief was that only the worthy made As, and every educator knew, when they started a new school year, that some students would fail. This may no longer be the expectation, but in the movement to "every child will learn," many worry that grades are inflated, that standards are not rigorous enough.

The reality is that the world changed but the measuring stick did not. Not so long ago the world had a place for those students who were "not the academic type." Those students could leave school, without a diploma, and still find a reasonable level of employment. The fact that some students did not make the cut did not seem so bad. Obviously, this is no longer the case.

Schools today have the responsibility to make sure that *every* student finishes school with a diploma, and in most states they all have to finish in the same amount of time *and* be ready for postsecondary training. This means that the learning is no longer optional. It also means that the difficult students, the ones who don't just sail through school, the ones who used to drop out, are still there, but teachers have to get them through school successfully, too.

This changes the whole dynamic of teaching, but it really changes grading. It is no longer possible to just keep using a bell curve mentality. It is no longer okay for some students to fail. It is imperative to find new ways of thinking about how schools assess students.

This is the point at which many commentators on the current state of education in the United States begin to weep and wail and gnash their teeth. Schools are failing, and the United States is being left behind! Quick, do something!

Ridiculous! Do not believe that for one second! It is all too easy to look back through rose-colored glasses to an imaginary past, when all students were well-groomed, well-fed, and above average, but is that what really happened? A fairly cursory review of the state of education would tell otherwise.

Education in the United States is not worse today than it was in the past. Schools, especially public schools, are doing more than ever before—and more, in fact, than any educational system has ever attempted in the recorded history of the planet! These United States are attempting to (no, we're not there yet, but we are attempting to!) educate every child in one of the largest, most diverse countries in human history.

Listen to that: *Every child*, the rich ones, the poor ones, the white ones, the non-white ones, the urban, suburban, and rural ones, the children of families that trace their heritage back to pre-Columbian America, Jamestown, slavery, legal immigration, illegal immigration; the ones who read before they begin school, the ones who are nonverbal. American schools are attempting to give every one of these children the skills they need to successfully pursue a postsecondary education.

Have all schools figured out how to do that completely successfully yet? Of course not. There will always be room for improvement. Are the gaps between the effective schools and the failing schools way too big? Absolutely! Can professional educators and public policy makers continue with the status quo? No!

However, before schools are condemned on all fronts, it may be wise to consider this. In many average districts, the lowest math class that is offered at the freshman level is Algebra. One short generation ago, Algebra was the class in which many students ended their formal mathematics training, not the one they began in! How then can anyone reasonably make the claim that schools have not made progress? And this is just one example!

It is easy for those outside—and those inside—the field of public education to bemoan the state of education in America. As noted, there is great room for improvement in many districts. To use the shortcomings to completely reject the gains that schools have made is as shortsighted as denying that shortcomings exist.

Okay, time to get off the soapbox and back to the grading discussion. The old model of the bell curve just won't work anymore. It is no longer possible to allow *any* student to fail. Learning cannot be optional. This does not mean that the grading template outlined at the beginning of the chapter won't work; it does mean, however, that those who issue grades need to step back and take a hard look. It also means that when a student lands in the D or F categories, more steps will be needed to help that student.

The upside is that if the advice given in the last chapter is heeded, teachers will quit recording grades for the work that students do in order to learn the material. In that case, there are no grades artificially lowered on the basis of what was "turned in." If teachers are only grading student performance on summative assessments, the grade will actually reflect authentic student learning.

The question now becomes, what happens when the students don't learn the material in the time allotted? The answer to that question in the past was that the student had to just keep going. That won't get it anymore! Passing students on without the requisite skills is, thankfully, no longer acceptable. If the old model is no longer working, it is time to develop a new model, and that can be hard.

Whenever a problem seems intractable, it is useful to go back and review. The problem is that classrooms have students who are failing. What does that mean for teachers? Reviewing the definition developed at the beginning of this chapter for a D or an F, it is clear that those students have big gaps in, or have not at all learned, the material that the teacher felt (based on curriculum, state standards, etc.) that they should have learned.

The next step is to ask, why? If a large number of students have not learned the material, then the teacher has to review his own delivery of instruction. Was the teacher clear about what he wanted students to know? Was the material thoroughly taught? Were the questions asked of students coherently?

The key here is to be very clear about what the teacher wanted the students to know. This is why the personal outline that the teacher develops to organize the objectives to be taught is so critical. If the teacher can't clearly identify what he wants the students to know, chances are the students won't be able to identify that information, either.

If the answer to any of these questions is that the instruction was not appropriate or sufficient, then it is the teacher's responsibility to "fix" what he, the teacher, got wrong. This can be really hard for some teachers. Sometimes teachers fall into the trap of infallibility. If the teacher admits to being less than perfect, how will the students react? It turns out that most students will respect a teacher even more when the teacher can admit to being less than perfect.

Not only can he earn respect, but the teacher who admits to having a less-than-perfect lesson is modeling real-life problem-solving skills. A failed (or if that seems too harsh, a "less-than-perfect") lesson can happen to anyone. Educators teach students valuable lessons when they teach students to go back and try again.

Whether or not the teacher is ready to acknowledge a fault in his own instruction, there is just no ethical way around re-teaching. If just a few students did not master the material, there are manageable ways to address remediation. But teachers who try to remediate with large numbers of students are going to quickly find themselves overwhelmed and frustrated.

What if only a few students failed to learn the material? This calls for more investigation, and there is no single answer. It is necessary to go deeper, to look for causes and find the holes. Usually they are not hard to find: The student had a bad day, the student missed class, the student has a learning problem (diagnosed or undiagnosed) that was not taken into account, and the list goes on.

Whatever the case, learning is still not optional. The teacher is going to need to do some problem-solving—maybe with the student, maybe with other teachers of the same student—to create a plan to help the student learn. In today's educational environment, the teacher needs to remediate.

This almost always sounds more complicated than it turns out to be. Oh sure, easy to say, but really, think about it. After an individual review of each student who struggled on a task, the answer to why each student struggled is usually obvious. Remember, this should only be a small number of students; if lots of students are not being successful, the teacher is going to have to review his own practices.

If many students are not learning—careful, that is *learning*, not failing to turn in homework—then go back to the instructional side and make changes there. If, on the other hand, only a few students need remediation, the problem is much more manageable. Once the focus for remediation has narrowed to just a few students, solutions are not nearly as big of a challenge.

This is not to say that all students *will* be successful. This statement has been put into print, in this book, with a certain amount of hesitation. Every educator has met the teacher who takes a statement like this and uses it to cover his own ineffectiveness. It is sad but true that some of the most ineffective teachers either cannot or will not look to their own practices, and instead blame the students for the lack of student success. That is not the intention here.

Hopefully it is safe to assume that those who are bothering to read a book about how to improve teaching, and have made it all the way to Chapter 5, are not going to take these words and twist them so intentionally. So the admission that teachers and schools are not going to be successful with every student deserves to be said.

It would be wonderful to believe that every single student in a given class will be successful. It would be equally lovely to believe that after teachers read this book, all of the students in all of their classes will be successful. The truth is that students are human beings, not widgets. Human beings are remarkable, both in their potential and in their individuality.

We may deeply believe that all students can learn, and not only *can*, but *want to*, learn. However, as human beings, each student comes to the table with his or her own individual needs and sometimes baggage. At the end of the day (or the school year), all any teacher can do is her best to give students every opportunity to find success in the classroom.

The question of whether every child can be successful is a tricky one. It's tricky because no matter how much educators may want to save them all, that may just not always be possible. The bottom line is this: Teachers and schools must operate under the belief that every child can learn. Every child deserves that chance.

In reviewing grading and grading practices, another area that is instructive to rethink is the attitude toward assignment due dates. It may have been popular, once, to believe that rigorous teachers had fair but firm due dates with significant consequences for late work. After all, how could we teach students personal responsibility if we did not require students to turn in assignments on time?

The problem with firm due dates is that they do not meet the logic test with regard to assessing a student's learning. Look at it in light of the discussion of grades in the previous chapter. The whole "do it or else" threat only works if the "or else" is something that the receiver views as negative. And not only negative, but worse than the alternative.

It has already been established that many of the students who are the object of this kind of motivation are not motivated by grades in the first place. Oh sure, the good kid who already makes straight As is motivated, but not the kid who isn't turning in her work. Unfortunately, that kid would rather take a whole bucket of Fs than write the required essay. That student has learned that if she just keeps procrastinating, dawdling, losing the rough draft, etc., eventually the teacher will give up, give her the F, and move on.

If teachers really want to give that student a meaningful consequence, a negative consequence, then the teacher needs to insist that she do the work. Well then, the old school aficionados will say, at least the student should get points off for turning it in late! Really? Explain that to a parent.

Susie didn't want to do the assignment in the first place, the parent finally got her to do it, and still Susie receives a poor, or worse, a failing grade because the work was turned in past the deadline? That will certainly get Susie to work harder next time! Does anyone really believe that? Even so, it brings the argument right back to the grade not being about ability, but rather about task completion. In this scenario, the teacher is grading promptness, not learning.

But the counterargument, from the old school crowd, is that it's not fair if Susie gets more time than the others to do the work. This argument doesn't stand up to scrutiny, either. In the first place, treating every student in exactly the same way is hardly fair. In the second place, the grade should be a reflection of the learning itself, not the time it took to acquire the learning. What is "fair" can get tricky fast, since any student may need individual treatment and help at any particular time.

Good teachers don't hesitate to give individual students extensions when they are in a car accident or have a tragedy, do they? If it is reasonable to provide some exceptions, then to treat all students exactly the same at every moment isn't realistic. Don't schools want to give students the help they need, hopefully when they need it? What about individualization, learning styles, and the like?

Does every student need the same amount of instruction? What about providing students with remediation—is it fair if they get extra help? What isn't fair is the premise that every student is expected to do the same amount of learning, at the same rate, for the same duration. Just because the schools of the past were put together in an assembly-line fashion does not mean that in the twenty-first century this model should be perpetuated.

Educators, sometimes unwittingly, accept this expectation of equality among students without thinking through the realities. In the first place, students start school with wildly different foundations, including whether or not they have books in their homes, have adequate nutrition, or have the same level of parental support.

In the second place, and more importantly, consider the goal of effective schools. If the goal is to do everything that can be done to help every student learn, then the learning is the constant and the time it takes to achieve that goal should be the variable. Unfortunately, using time as a variable is a great idea, but not all that practical in most schools. One of the only options classroom teachers have to vary time is to be flexible with due dates.

Now it is time to tackle a subject that can generate some heat with regard to grades: homework. There are countless studies that have been conducted about the value of homework. Of course, this is not just any homework, but rather homework that provides the student with the opportunity to independently practice the material.

There is no disputing the value of homework in the abstract. As a theory it is difficult to argue with its value. The actual implementation of homework, however, is another story, and a place where theory and practice collide rather than intersect.

Upon deeper reflection, it seems that there are few things in schools, especially public schools, that separate the "haves" from the "have-nots" as much as homework. Many children, most notably the children of educators, have a distinct advantage. They have nice, middle-class homes to go to. They are asked, by an adult, on a daily basis, whether or not they have homework. They are encouraged (usually required) to complete the assigned homework. They are provided with an appropriate setting in which to do their homework, and if necessary, they are given help with that homework.

Now think about some of the students whom teachers encounter in their classrooms every day. In too many schools, there are kids who come from poverty, maybe deep poverty. These students often come home to an empty house, apartment, or trailer. No one is there to ask about homework. Many times these children live in single-parent households with a parent who is working two jobs just to get by. Sometimes the parents themselves did not graduate from high school.

These parents may not be in a position to offer help to their children. Even if they have the energy, they may not have the academic background. In too many places, students come to school and report that the police were at the home the previous night because Mom's boyfriend was drunk and beat her up and they had to call the cops, or some other equally horrible story.

Now, in her enthusiasm to raise academic standards in her classroom, the teacher asks these students for their homework. Really? Think about how this plays to these students! They have all this turmoil in their life, they may or may not have even had a decent meal, they may or may not have clean clothes to wear, and all the teacher seems to care about is their homework.

Is homework really high on such a student's priority list? From an emotional perspective, does that child really need one more reason to feel inadequate?

Homework is great if all the kids do it, if they do it correctly, and if it is used as an extension of the learning. Again, the research is clear: homework has a positive correlation to student achievement. This is not an indictment of the concept of homework.

However, the reality in which many schools find themselves is that this idyll is just not the case. The teachers in schools with these conditions of poverty have enough problems trying to differentiate the instruction that happens in their room, juggling the kids who finish first from the ones who finish last, let alone adding more disparity to the situation.

The takeaway from this is not an endorsement of homework, nor a denunciation of homework. The key here is for teachers to be thoughtful and reflective about their student population. The question teachers need to consider with any activity is this: *Will this activity get my students closer or further away from the goal—learning?*

On a related note, it sounds great to utilize a new application of technology that is the latest in educational innovation. "Flipped classrooms" can be a great idea. Teachers record the lecture part of the lesson and upload it to a website. Students can then access this at home through the Internet. Class time is then used for that the portion of the lesson usually given as homework while teachers are present to assist as needed.

This sounds great, but again, there should be no doubt that lots of students, or even schools for that matter, don't have the capacity to do this. What's more, it should be taken as a given that some smart little guys will use the excuse "the Internet was down" for not having done the work. If there are teachers who can use technology this way, more power to them, but not all good teachers will be able to make this work.

Again, it is not that homework is bad, but the use of homework, without a very clear assessment of the goals, can be disastrous. After all, what is the rationale for homework in the first place?

Homework should be something that increases the student's understanding of the material that has been taught. Homework should be something that students have enough familiarity with to be able to complete without assistance.

The last thing teachers want is for students to go home and practice something incorrectly. Un-teaching that which has been practiced incorrectly and then re-teaching the material takes everyone further away from the goal, not closer to it. If the problems caused by homework outweigh the benefits that students derive from it . . . does it make sense from a purely cost-benefit perspective?

So if a teacher doesn't give homework, and she doesn't give grades for the work that is done in class, then what does get graded? How should a teacher assess a student's progress through the curriculum? What do grades look like when curriculum, instruction, and feedback work together?

One teacher's answer is to grade only two types of work: Document-Based Questions and Tests. This should not be considered a template for every classroom; it is merely an example. It allows the teacher to provide students, parents, administrators, and others with an accurate assessment of what the students know and can do. What is important is not the category itself, but the rationale the teacher has thought through to justify its inclusion.

Writing assignments are important in every discipline. If reading and writing are not just skills for English or Communication Arts class, then all disciplines need to be asking students to engage in reading and writing. Writing assignments make it easy to give individual instruction to each student based on the level of their individual performance, but only if teachers spend time working with individual students.

Document-Based Questions (DBQs) are a new addition in many classrooms. The teacher in this example uses a modified version adapted for eighth-grade students. Since the current focus in instruction is on implementing rigorous standards, DBQs can be a great instructional tool.

This teacher gives the students a paragraph, from a primary source document if it is appropriate to the curriculum. Students are then asked to answer a question that requires an understanding of the passage. The grading expectations are clearly communicated to the students before they began.

Ideally, the document should be related to the topic that is being studied, but it should be something that has *not* been explicitly taught. The only way for students to be able to answer the question should be by reading the paragraph. In this way, the student's ability to read and comprehend a passage can be directly assessed without the influence of prior knowledge.

The teacher in this example required student responses to be two to three sentences in length. Students were graded not only on content, but also on all the conventions of formal writing. This then assesses both the student's ability to read and to comprehend a passage, as well as the student's ability to write independently using the writing process.

Student responses were then graded on a traditional A to F scale. In this way, the grading definitions that were detailed at the beginning of this chapter actually become an accurate reflection of what the student can produce.

One caveat, an F is 50 percent—not zero. This is important for two reasons: If the student makes an attempt, it gives them credit for the attempt. It also prevents an F from becoming a disproportionate drag on the student's overall grade. Think for a moment about the difference between 0/10 and 5/10: Both are Fs.

This teacher also gave a more traditional summative assessment or test. Tests are just that: end-of-unit assessments. These will be addressed in detail in the next chapter, so for now let's just say that tests are obviously a component of grading.

In this example, the final student grade is a much more accurate reflection of what that student knows and can do. The grading structure is based on the final products the student creates. When the teacher reports this grade, the parent, as well as the student, has a clear idea of how the student measures in relation to the learning the teacher intended.

Grading is a complicated component of what schools do. Grades may seem simple at first, but when digging into how grades are determined and what they represent, we see that they are anything but simple. The examples in this chapter are only one way to assess grades and the reasons they are assessed. In the end, *what* is graded is not nearly as important as *why* it is graded.

This is not to advocate that everyone assess grades in the same way. What is being advocated is that teachers give some serious thought to exactly what they grade and why. Thinking deeply about what the grades mean and how grades are arrived at can change the way teachers view everything else.

If instruction is the component of the educational universe that is most public for teachers, grades hold the same importance to students. The whole idea of a "grade" is used so casually, by so many people, that it can easily be taken for granted. It is critically important for schools to be very clear about how grades are determined.

The non-educational world, the world schools prepare students for, believes that it knows what grades mean. An A is good, and an F is bad—but it is more than that. When a student receives an A, she is assumed to have a level of knowledge. When a student receives an F, she is assumed to lack that knowledge.

Too many extraneous criteria have been rolled into grading. This results in confusion for those outside of schools. When students fail courses because they turned work in late, needed more time to acquire a concept, or did not complete classwork, is a low grade an accurate reflection of what they have actually learned? What do these kinds of grades say about the teacher's responsibility to help students learn, not just have teachers teach?

To be effective at preparing all students for the world after school, it is necessary for teachers to reexamine how and what grades are. Grades need to flow directly from what students should know (curriculum), through how students are taught (instruction), and result in an accurate reflection of what the students have learned (grades).

Again, back to the recurring theme of this book: When all of the various pieces of what teachers do work together, the result is gratifying. To make schools that get it right, that work, grading practices are certainly an integral component, and one that certainly requires a closer look.

KEY IDEAS TO REMEMBER

- Even though students are categorized and judged based upon the grades they have received, there is no true standard by which those grades are determined.
- The bell curve model, which judges the bottom of the curve as failing, is no longer acceptable in the modern era of education. All students are

- expected to learn, and merely sorting students out will not serve this purpose.
- Effective classrooms, and schools, must have processes that address those students who have not met the expectations. Merely assigning a failing grade to the student is no longer a sufficient response.
- Every child deserves the chance to learn and also the chance to have adults in their lives who will not give up if they don't get it the first time.
- Grades should reflect student learning; they are used to judge student proficiency with regard to the curriculum. They should not be a catch-all of effort, energy, timeliness, etc.
- Homework, while beneficial to many students, can have detrimental consequences for at-risk populations. Teachers need to be aware of the needs of the students in their classrooms and use discretion even when implementing research-based strategies.

QUESTIONS FOR FURTHER REFLECTION

- What does an A mean in your classroom/school? What does an F mean? Is the meaning the same for all teachers in your building? What are the implications?
- What happens when a student fails in your classroom/school? What steps are in place to prevent failure?
- How do homework and other classroom practices impact individual students (the haves versus the have-nots) differently? Are there practices that increase the gap between students?

Chapter Six

Testing to Get Real Results

The last two chapters dealt with grading, so now it is time to talk about assessment, or testing. This is where the pieces really start to come together, and it is one of the main ideas behind the writing of this book in the first place.

A review of the books currently on the market that address ways to improve education shows that most of these books are very targeted. It seems that much of the literature in the field has a narrow focus. There are countless books on curriculum, on instruction, on assessment, on every other facet of teaching, but very little has been written that takes a comprehensive look at all of teaching as a whole.

There is great power in having the pieces of any system work together. To reiterate, in the same way that it is possible to develop a synergy when a group of people work together and collaborate as professionals, it is equally powerful when the components of teaching work together. This kind of positive interaction can make what happens in the classroom more effective than the sum of the parts. Testing what has been taught is where educators can see this synergy in action.

Think about the progression this book has taken from the beginning. First, we took a look at what was being taught, developing a clear idea of what students should know and be able to do. Then we explored how to promote student learning through instruction, including ways to measure their progress along the way in the form of feedback that was termed grading. Now comes the proverbial place where the rubber meets the road: the test.

The language used in this chapter is purposely about testing and not assessment in order to be clear in differentiating between the forms that assessment can take. Assessment is really everything that teachers do to give students feedback. Most of the last two chapters addressed this continuous kind of feedback, which is characterized these days as formative assessment.

Now it is time to focus on the summative part of feedback, which has traditionally been called testing. This is usually the paper/pencil work that students do at the end of a teaching cycle. It is what students worry about (the teacher hopes), what parents look at, and for those who read the last two chapters, the component on which the majority of the grade in the class should really be based.

What, then, is the purpose of a test? If a teacher is following the pattern outlined in this book, at the very least the test is the only thing left with which to determine a grade. The test should certainly be more than just a grade. The test really is where the rubber meets the road.

Let's review: The school district is given authority by the state, through the local school board, to teach the children in a geographical area (at least in public schools). The school board uses state mandates to develop and approve curriculum for every area of study in the district. Teachers are hired to instruct students, with the goal of providing students with opportunities by which they will achieve a level of competence with regard to those curricular goals.

Therefore, if the goal of the school and the teacher is to ensure that students gain competence in the areas outlined in the curriculum, the test is the instrument that is used to measure that competence. So, who is the test measuring, the students or the teacher? The answer, really, is both.

When many of those in the field today started teaching, "back in the day," as students would say, they gave tests that looked just like the tests that their cooperating teacher gave when they were student teaching. These tests often followed a similar format: multiple-choice items, matching items, maybe some true/false items, and a couple of essay questions. This seemed like a balanced approach, it seemed fair, and it looked familiar, so young teachers went on their merry way.

At this point it seems necessary to stop and tell a story—a true story—about Mike. Mike was a freshman in high school, a good-looking kid, not particularly interested in academics, and fairly significantly learning disabled. Mike paid attention, usually, but he didn't act like he cared about his grades, and consequently he routinely received failing grades on the tests.

Mike would guess on the objective parts, skip the essays completely, and, not surprisingly, fail every test. Mike's normal grade on a test was a 30 percent. Then came the day when his teacher, as she sat to create the next test, got stuck. This young teacher simply could not come up with any objective questions that did not qualify as trivia questions. She had lots of interesting essay questions, but that was it. So the teacher took a deep breath and told her students that she was really sorry, but she was going to give an all-essay test.

In an attempt to calm their fears, she told them she would let them choose to answer only five questions from the list of ten provided. The students, predictably, groaned and took the test. Imagine this young teacher's surprise when she graded Mike's test; he got all five questions right, a 100 percent!

What happened next changed this teacher's life. When she gave the students back their tests, Mike looked at her, his eyes wide with wonder, and he said, "I'm not stupid!" Stab the teacher in the heart with a knife! All this time Mike thought that his grade was a reflection of his intellect. Mike thought that his low test scores meant that he was dumb.

It turns out that Mike was like many underachieving students. It doesn't take many experiences of trying and failing before they realize that failing hurts. Many students have taken refuge in passive-aggressive avoidance behaviors. They make a minimal attempt to complete a test and when they fail, as they are sure to do with such a minimal effort, they shrug off the whole exercise as a waste of their time. This way they can comfort themselves with the idea that they are not "stupid," but rather it is the test that is "stupid."

Once Mike was unable to give his usual minimal effort, guessing at the objective items and skipping the essays, his real knowledge of the material was displayed. It turns out that Mike had learned more than he thought he did. It also became apparent that although Mike was using avoidance to protect himself from the hurt of failure, in reality, Mike had come to believe that the F he regularly received was, indeed, all he was capable of. The young teacher never gave another objective test again.

Why did Mike, who skipped the essay portion of the usual test, do the essays on this test? It turns out that while students may put forth no effort whatsoever to answer objective items correctly, those same students are very reluctant to turn in a blank piece of paper. They hide behind carelessly completed work to maintain the appearance of playing along.

Once Mike had to actually write down answers, he found it easier to write what he knew about the question. It seems that making up a wrong answer takes a lot more effort than recalling information, especially if the information really is there.

Objective tests sound appealing. "Objective." It just sounds right. No teacher bias, just an "objective" look at what students have learned. But Mike's story invites teachers to start thinking. What does a teacher really know about their student's learning from those objective tests? Turns out, teachers don't know much at all.

If a student gets a multiple-choice question right, does that mean that they learned the material or just that they were lucky in their guess? The other problem with objective tests is that they almost always test at low levels on the Depth of Knowledge scale. Most classroom teachers just don't have the background to construct higher-level objective items. To really be skilled at constructing higher-level multiple-choice questions may require a master's degree in tests and measurements.

Factor in the reality that objective tests rely heavily on the student's ability to read. Of course, students need to be able to read, but many objective test items are constructed in such a way as to trick students. The student needs to be able to read the items not only for comprehension, but also with a high degree of specificity, since the incorrect answers are often designed to be subtle in their errors.

If the test is really a test of reading and not the specific curricular objectives, then what does a low score on such a test reveal? Is it possible for a student to have at least a moderate grasp of the curricular material, but be unable to demonstrate that knowledge if they are a struggling reader? If failing test scores require that student to retake the course, will further exposure to the material they already know improve their reading score and thereby the test grade?

How many teachers have seen long, complicated packets of questions, asking students to recall a series of facts that may or may not be related to any curricular objectives, passed off by colleagues as tests? It may seem as if such teachers feel that the rigor of the test has a direct correlation to the gross weight of the packet. Does this really measure what a student has learned about the material mandated by the curriculum?

No, scanning machines won't grade them, but just a little reflection will reinforce the value of the essay or short answer format. It is certainly a more accurate way to assess what students have, or have not, learned in class.

Since most content areas are only trying to determine a student's content knowledge of specific curriculum, a short answer type of test does not need to be graded for anything other than content knowledge. A bonus is that this allows the teacher to differentiate for students with disabilities; bulleted lists or sentence fragments demonstrate what students know about the material just as accurately as well-constructed written responses.

Okay, so if a teacher decides to give an essay or short answer test, what source can they use to find the questions? Although it may be tempting, it is advisable to avoid the tests that come with the textbook. In the first place, these are usually largely objective items, and after hearing Mike's story, who can bring themselves to do that to another student?

The other problem with the textbook-created test is that it is naturally limited to just the material that was covered in that book. A review of the discussion from the second chapter will remind the reader that the task is to teach students the material in the curriculum, which hopefully is not just a list of the table of contents of the textbook.

Aha! This is the answer to where the test questions come from: They come from the curriculum itself. Like many of the things discussed in this book, this sounds terribly obvious. Sadly, what is obvious can be easily overlooked.

If what teachers want is for students to learn the information that is identified in the curriculum, then it stands to reason that teachers should be testing students over that material. In fact, if the objective items are also in the curriculum outline plan that the teacher created in Chapter 2, it is easy to just take the objectives and turn them into questions.

To make this an even prettier package, develop these questions before the teaching even begins! What could be more straightforward than to be clear about what students should know, then to teach them that material, and then to check to see if they learned it? This is the ultimate in teaching to the test. It is so simple, but how often do educators miss this so completely?

Want to make this an even more completely integrated, elegant package? Use the objective items that have been turned into questions as an introduction to each class. Post the question on the board at the beginning of class. Students will understand these much better than those horrible postings so many teachers feel forced to use. "The student will . . ."

Want to impress an administrator? Post the day's objective as a question on the board at the beginning of class. Teach the class in engaging ways that help students really learn. Then, at the end of class, ask the students to go back and answer the question on an exit card and hand it to the teacher as they leave. It doesn't get more targeted than that.

Teachers tie themselves up into knots with complicated curriculum, with endless lists of objectives. They fill page after page in lesson plan books with elaborate instructional tactics, and they create lengthy tests, complete with in-depth study guides. What would happen if curriculum were simplified into the big ideas? What if teachers then created a series of activities that would provide students with ways to develop an understanding of those ideas and then asked students to explain what they had learned?

Another trick that comes from Mike's story is to give students choices on the test. Give students eight to ten questions, but have them choose the four to five that they answer. When the teacher in the story made the decision to give the class an all-essay test, she was worried that they would revolt, so she tried to "ease the pain" by allowing the students to choose which questions to answer. Turns out, this works great!

In the first place, it makes the test higher level just in the format itself. If students have to know what they know (meta-cognition), they are demonstrating a higher level of understanding. Having an awareness of what you know is a much more complex level of understanding than simply attempting to answer every question that is fed to you.

One suggestion: Do not allow students to just answer all the questions and then only "count" the correct answers. This negates the benefit. Instead, tell students that only the number of required answers (i.e., five of ten) will even be read by the teacher. This forces students to make assessments about their own learning, to know what they know, to be aware of what they have learned.

Another benefit to allowing students to have this choice is that it is a great strategy to help students with test anxiety. If students feel that they have some level of control, it calms their worry about forgetting something. For the same reason, allow students to answer the questions in any order they like. If a student can have success on the first item they attempt, by answering a question they feel comfortable with, they have a much better chance at being successful throughout the entire test.

Oftentimes students who think they have forgotten everything suddenly remember what they learned once they get started, since the test gets their juices flowing. Another bonus is that it is almost impossible for students to copy off of each other while testing. No two students choose the same items in the same order, and so they can't casually copy.

Additionally, creating tests with such a limited number of open-ended questions makes it much more realistic for the average classroom teacher to incorporate the appropriate level of rigor. It was noted above that most teachers are not sufficiently trained in tests and measurements to be able to successfully create higher-level multiple-choice questions.

Creating higher-order thinking questions in an open-ended format is much easier. Higher-level essay questions are relatively easy to produce. Find that old Bloom's Taxonomy chart or a Depth of Knowledge chart. Use those high-level stem words, and it is easy to make sure that the questions are assessing students at a high level of rigor.

Since most teachers are only looking for the student's content knowledge on the test, they find that they don't need to grade tests for grammar, spelling, etc. Make no mistake, good writing is important in every content area, which is why including specific writing assignments as a regular part of teaching is vitally important. These writing assignments should not only be scored for content but also for style, syntax, grammar, and the conventions of formal writing.

However, separating out what is being assessed, content versus style, can be a really important distinction on an assessment. The impulse to over-grade is what too often causes teachers problems with grading. If everything is included, the teacher can have a hard time identifying exactly what has or has not been learned. (More on this in the next chapter.)

As with everything that has been included in this book, these practices are in no way the only right way to get the job done, or necessarily even the best way. It is important, however, for every teacher to know exactly why they are doing the things that they do. It is absolutely necessary to know what you are trying to accomplish. Each teacher needs to thoroughly examine her own practices and take a critical look at what she is doing and why. This type of reflection is what, more often than not, separates effective classrooms from ineffective ones.

One of the biggest advantages to testing in this way is evident when it is time to remediate for those students who demonstrate that they have not learned what the teacher wanted them to learn. Ah, *remediation*, another word that has changed the way modern teachers approach teaching.

The last chapter went into some detail on this subject. Back in the day, kids either passed or failed. Teachers didn't spend much time remediating. Now, rightly so, student failure is not an option. What do teachers do when students don't learn? If the test comes directly from the curriculum, and it reflects exactly what students need to know and what they learned, when students are not successful, it means that they have not acquired the knowledge that is essential.

The good news for teachers is that because of the essay format, there really is no need to change the test if students need to retake it. It turns out that if students don't know the material, no amount of exposure to the question itself will change that. As hard as it may be to believe, students can literally be given the exact questions before the test and still be unable to answer them correctly—if they did not learn the material. Since students have to explain themselves on an essay test, simply memorizing facts is usually insufficient.

Since failure should not be an option, students who do not score at least 70 percent on a test are the students who require remediation. One way to begin the process of remediation is to require those students with a 70 percent or lower grade to retake the test.

It would seem that once a student had already taken the test, retaking the same test would be easy. However, it turns out that if he doesn't work to actually learn the material, he will do poorly *every time he takes it*. A teacher once (only once, he insists) had a student fail the exact same test four times in a row! After the fourth time, the student turned to the teacher and said, "Maybe I should study?" The teacher solemnly agreed. The fifth time she earned a 100 percent.

What can quickly become clear is that, often, a failing grade on the test does not automatically mean that a student needs a great deal of remediation. Most of the time, when a student scores below a 70 percent and retakes the quiz, they earn an 80 percent or higher on the retake. This could be because they have already seen the test, but maybe they just had a bad day when they took the test the first time.

Educators are fond of saying that every student can learn, and hopefully all teachers believe this. Teachers are also fond of saying that not every student should be expected to learn the same amount, in the same period of time. Just maybe, some students need more than one exposure to the material to really learn it. If taking the test twice helps these students to learn what the teacher is trying to teach them . . . wasn't that the goal in the first place?

What about the student who still fails to reach an acceptable score on the second try? That student will need some additional, individual remediation. It turns out that when teachers have their classes set up in this way, the number of students failing multiple times is so small that providing some one-on-one to the struggling student isn't all that hard to do.

Teachers often spend lots of time worrying about how they will find time to re-teach those students who require it. The reality is that for most teachers, the number of students who really don't understand the material after it has been taught in engaging ways, and assessed as described above, is remarkably low.

When is all this retesting supposed to happen? Having students retesting while the other students move on in the curriculum just causes that student who is already struggling to miss even more of the instruction. Consider having students come in and do retakes on "their" time, such as at lunch or before school.

When students are required to give up something of value to themselves in order to move on in the curriculum, it teaches them responsibility. This is the lesson teachers think they are providing to students with a low or failing grade. The difference is, as laid out in the last chapter, these are often the students who are not motivated by grades in the first place. Making students accountable with their own time will keep students from gaming the system by not studying the first time and simply retaking the test if the grade was poor.

Another advantage to scheduling retakes in this way is that it allows any student to retake the test to improve their grade. All those teachers who thought that giving "late work" students deadline extensions was unfair to those students who turned their work in on time should love this idea.

If the highly motivated students also have the opportunity to retake a test, this certainly seems more equitable than only allowing that opportunity to those who failed. It also allows every single student the opportunity to earn whatever grade they want to work hard enough for. Parents love this and are almost universally supportive.

One last question remains when considering this way of addressing testing, and unfortunately there may not be a completely satisfactory answer for this one. The question becomes: Do students need to take objective tests in order to be prepared for the objective sections of the state test?

Many teachers have mixed feelings on this one, and there does not seem to be much research in this particular area to guide practice. It seems clear from the discussion at the beginning of this chapter that it is difficult to gain a true understanding of a student's level of understanding from any objective test that a teacher could create or, for that matter, administer.

If a student answers an objective item correctly, is it because they knew the answer or because they guessed correctly? If a student answers incorrectly, is it because they did not know the material, or because they did not or could not read the question accurately, or just because they guessed? If no one gains any useful information, then what is the value of the testing?

If a teacher assesses his students' ability to read various types of material on the Document-Based Questions that were discussed in Chapter 5; and on the student's ability to answer individual curriculum-based questions on the tests, are those students not better prepared to perform on the high-stakes test? At least the teacher can have some confidence that the students know the content and can read material related to that content.

One teacher's answer to this concern is to incorporate objective, multiple-choice questions into the DBQ. This teacher does not even include the student's scores on these items in the calculation of the student's grade. By adding just a few multiple-choice items to the existing DBQ, the teacher gives students the opportunity to practice reading multiple-choice items. The teacher also uses these items to train students in test-taking strategies, like how to read carefully and not just skim.

There is no easy, clear-cut answer to the question of using objective items just to have students practice. It is up to each teacher to make those decisions for their own students based on what they see as a need in their own classrooms. (More on how to collect and use data so that teachers can make reasonable decisions about questions like these, in the next chapter.)

Testing is a huge part of what teachers do. It is, and should be, the way that teachers can judge their own effectiveness as instructors and the way that teachers judge the competence of students. Testing emphatically does *not* need to be the area in which teachers just continue to muddle along with the same old, same old way that has always been done.

Testing needs to be a genuinely integrated part of the whole that effective teachers can create. Starting with the curriculum, through instruction and formative assessment, teachers need to create a clear and coherent thread that culminates with testing, and not just march forward through curriculum.

If students learning, and not just teachers teaching, is the goal of schools, it becomes essential for teachers to have valid means to assess what each student has really learned. The test, then, holds a central place in effective classrooms. It is the pivotal piece of information that allows all of the stakeholders in schools to have confidence in the preparation of students. The test is so much more important than just an ending to a unit of study.

Teachers need to move backward from the test and look at instruction and formative assessment with an eye toward how students will be assessed at the end. Creating that synergy between the pieces of the process of teaching will move schools from places where curriculum is merely covered, to places where students actually build meaning for themselves.

KEY IDEAS TO REMEMBER

- Objective tests may not be as objective as a teacher believes. The content of the questions remains subjective on the part of the teacher.
- Objective tests alone give very little information with regard to student mastery of curriculum. Without deeper inquiry, it is impossible to know whether students answered correctly from knowledge or lucky guessing.
- The purpose of the end-of-chapter/unit test is to assess whether or not the students mastered the curriculum being taught in that chapter/unit. The test should allow students to demonstrate what they have learned.
- When students do not demonstrate a mastery of the curriculum, they require remediation; learning cannot be optional.
- Testing is the pivotal piece of information that allows all of the stakeholders in schools to have confidence in the preparation of students; it confirms student mastery of the curriculum that was taught.

QUESTIONS FOR FURTHER REFLECTION

- What is the relationship between curriculum and assessment in your classroom/school?
- How does your testing format provide you with information about your students' mastery of curricular objectives?
- What additional information would you like to have about your students' learning in your classroom/school?

Chapter Seven

Data Makes the Difference

Exploring the whole spectrum of the teaching process from curriculum to assessment is a lot to digest. While none of what appears here is particularly new, hopefully it has provided some new ways to think about old ideas. This next topic is not necessarily new, either, but it may seem so to some because it is usually the least familiar to classroom teachers. That topic is data.

It's not that teachers aren't familiar with data. For goodness' sake, schools generate enough data to satisfy the most ardent researcher. It's that practicing classroom teachers don't always know what to do with the data they generate. It can become overwhelming very quickly, and so, too often, classroom teachers either do not actively collect data or they are not able to analyze what they do collect with any success.

The biggest impediment to the use of data by those in the classroom is that teachers have a natural tendency to focus on individual students and rely on "gut checks" to determine whether goals are being met. This can be deadly in the big picture and can cause teachers to feel great frustration—that, in spite of their best efforts and all their hard work, they are not making any progress.

Teachers can focus so much on students who struggle that they can be left with the feeling that all students are struggling. What teacher is not more inclined to focus on the completely incorrect responses of two or three students than on the correct responses of the other twenty students?

This focus on the individual is not a bad thing; it is what classroom teachers are supposed to do. Teachers want to help kids. However, if teachers never back up and look at data in an objective way, they can never gain a true picture of what is working and what is not. As a matter of fact, without a good look at data, schools themselves often set out to solve the wrong problem.

As always, there is a story to illustrate this hard-earned lesson. This example comes from an administrator, not a teacher. In a large suburban high school, the building administration decided to try to focus on the freshman class, believing that if the school could address concerns at the very beginning, students would have a much better chance to move through high school and graduate on time. This seemed obvious, and with a great deal of enthusiasm the freshman principal spent the summer plotting out her approach.

As she reflected on the concerns that the freshman teachers had shared with her, she was determined to focus her attention in the area of attendance. It was common wisdom among freshman teachers that the problem at the freshman level was attendance. Teachers routinely lamented that poor attendance was the root cause of students earning Fs. Accordingly, the freshman principal planned attendance meetings with parents, with students, attendance contracts, all of the wonderful remedies that would help students be successful.

After the first grading period, she painstakingly gathered the data on numbers of students who had earned two or more Fs and on their attendance. She looked at all the data and groaned. How could she organize all this for seven hundred students in a way that would yield any useful information? So she started in the same place that most educators start, with averages.

It didn't take long to realize that averages told her nothing, so she backed up and plotted the data in a distribution chart. Wow! In no time at all, some very interesting things started to appear. An obvious pattern emerged and as she finished compiling the data, she learned to her surprise that something like 68 percent of the freshmen with two or more Fs had missed three days . . . or less. Less? . . . What?? That was not what anyone had thought was going on. All those who worked with the freshmen were sure that attendance was the problem, but the data did not support this conclusion.

Just to give closure to the story, yes, the students who missed lots of school were usually failing, but so were lots of other students who came to school every day. It turns out that the kids on the margins made up the bulk of the story and really needed attention, but since they were on the margins, they often didn't get the attention they needed.

A little reflection provided the answer. Take a nice kid, no overt issues, not a behavior problem, or a class clown, no attendance concerns, who passes tests but with low grades and turns in most of the homework. That kid is going to miss everybody's radar. They don't raise a flag on discipline, attendance, or failing test scores; they don't even hit the missing homework radar, since they turn in some of the work. But with a D on the test, and a couple of missed assignments, that kid slips below the line.

The kind of information that can be gained from data is critical. If the administrator in the story had spent that year focusing on attendance as a way to decrease student Fs she would have been sadly disappointed. She would have been fixing the wrong problem. Think how often this happens in schools. Everyone works their brains out with a fix they think will increase student achievement, and at the end of the year they see no change. The "gut check" is just not reliable.

What exactly is a "gut check"? It may be called by many names, but it is actually the development of a theory based on casual observation. Teachers spend the bulk of their time in schools every day, and they think they have their "finger on the pulse," they know why things happen. Using observation to determine the cause of a problem can be a good place to start, but this example shows how it can be misleading. Sometimes what gets one's attention is the unusual, not the commonplace. To really see the whole problem requires analysis beyond the "gut check."

School improvement work can be disheartening. It sometimes feels like everyone in the school works and works and yet nothing changes. No wonder so many teachers get burned out. Add to this the fact that many schools have reached the point at which the low fruit is gone, so to speak. The easy fixes have been made, and educators cannot rely on "gut checks" to make decisions anymore. Schools have to fix the problems they have, but first they have to know exactly where the problems lie.

The problem with collecting and analyzing data is that there just isn't that much help for the average teacher when it comes to knowing how to analyze classroom data. Not only are teachers rarely trained in the collection and analysis of data, they are most often going to have to make the effort on their own. Teachers will have to figure out for themselves what their own personal data tells them.

The good news is that once a teacher has worked through the data, and can see exactly where the problem lies, the plan to address the problem itself can become relatively obvious. Not every teacher is a data nerd who gets excited about what he learns from data. Nevertheless, it is exciting to see the data either reinforce a theory or lead in a completely new direction.

Another story: A middle-school teacher spent the summer thinking about what gaps he still had in his classroom. Most teachers do this to some degree. That is not to say that they spend every waking minute thinking about school, but teachers do think about what frustrations they have had or what areas they feel are not being focused on enough.

This middle-school teacher realized that although he had increased the amount of reading that students were doing in his class (the result of another summer's reflection), he really had no clear idea of each individual student's level of reading comprehension. Since this teacher did not teach reading directly, he felt inadequate to address the subject head-on.

The class did read lots of primary source excerpts and lots of historical fiction in the form of short stories, but they did all that reading together. The teacher regularly used that reading as a springboard for classroom discussions, and so the majority of that reading happened in the large group setting. This meant that the teacher was explaining to the students what they were reading as they went.

The teacher felt uncomfortable about forcing students to read aloud. He believed that the damage this could do to the shy and the self-conscious far outweighed the benefits. As he reflected, however, he realized that it was entirely possible for a student to sit in his class, pay attention, and not really be able to read independently at all. Clearly that was not okay, so he determined that he would address this over the course of the next school year.

As the teacher searched for a strategy to incorporate into his classroom to address reading comprehension, he remembered something he had seen his son do in his advanced classes. Advanced History classes are all about the DBQ, or Document-Based Question, which were introduced in a previous chapter.

When assigned a DBQ, students are given multiple documents and asked a question related to those documents. The students then have to use those documents to answer the question. There is obviously more to it than that, but the basic idea would work great for the teacher's goals.

By the way, doesn't this sound just like Common Core? Or other state-level assessments? Super! He realized he could kill two birds with one stone.

Even better, when the teacher got back to school and looked at the previous year's state test data, it confirmed a similar hole. Students across the board were tanking on the portion of the test where they were asked to demonstrate reading and writing skills in tandem.

So now the teacher knew what he need to do. He began by incorporating DBQ-type assessments into every unit. Easy, right? Not so fast. Just throwing a solution at a problem is not enough. Now he had to collect data to see if the strategy was working.

This is the step that is most often left out by classroom teachers. This is also the very mistake that prevents teachers from making the forward progress that they all work so hard for. Once an area of concern has been identified, then the teacher has to develop a strategy to address the concern. After the strategy has been implemented, it is critical to go back and look, as objectively as possible, to see whether or not the strategy actually impacted the concern in a positive way.

The teacher taught his students how to approach the DBQ. They completed one together, and the teacher modeled the thinking, reading, and writing steps that the students would need to use. Students were then given another example to work on their own.

Now what? The teacher had 120 student papers, but what to do with the numbers that were generated? This teacher started to analyze his data by doing what most teachers always do. He figured the average grade. On a scale of 1 to 10, the students had an average of 7. Okay, what did that mean? It didn't really tell anyone anything. Again, simple averages are rarely useful.

The teacher then went back and looked at individual student scores. The students whom he thought would do well, did well, and the students whom he expected to do poorly, did poorly. Again, this did not yield any new information. Finally, in exasperation, the teacher thought about what he wanted. He wanted all of his students to be proficient at reading a paragraph independently, to be able to pull the main idea out of the reading, and to be able to write a concise, logical answer to a question about the reading.

What the teacher wanted was a 9 or 10 out of 10 points. He reasoned that if a student scored an 8, they were nearing proficiency; if they scored a 7 to a 5, they were not where he wanted them to be, and so were basic. This sounded just like the categories on the state test! Perfect!

A side note: Be careful to only go down to a 5 and not a 0 in scoring. Five out of 10 is failing, but a score of 0 much more significantly impacts the final grade. As a matter of fact, it disproportionately affects a student's grade. Think about it, a 0/10 instead of a 5/10 gives a student, in essence, a double failing grade. By this logic, an A student should get 15/10!

The teacher went back to the individual student scores and put them into categories: 9–10 = proficient; 8 = nearing proficiency; 7–5 = basic. Then he graphed them (clearly he was a data nerd) so that he could see, over time, how students were doing. The teacher's goal was to get every student to proficient status by the end of the year.

Collecting concrete data is the starting point, but it is also important to graph the results. Often when teachers grade student papers, they feel very depressed. It sometimes seems like no progress is being made. When the results are graphed, especially over time, it is easier to see whether the trend line is moving in the right direction.

Another couple of side notes: The scientific among the readers of this work will readily see that the data collection described here has flaws. No two DBQs are exactly equivalent, and so the teacher is not testing the exact same variable all the time.

It is also important to recognize that expectations naturally increase over the course of the school year. What earned a student an 8 or a 9 in the beginning may no longer be the same as the student and teacher move through the year. This means that the data collection is imperfect and will not stand up to scientific scrutiny. This is okay: The goal for the average classroom teacher is not to publish research data in a scientific journal.

Clean data is not the real goal. The point of teachers collecting and analyzing students' scores is not to create a perfect research model. Don't misunderstand, there is nothing wrong with perfect research models. It is just not the goal of most classroom teachers to create perfect models. The average teacher has neither the expertise nor the inclination to create clean research.

The goal of data, for practicing teachers, is to increase their students' ability to read independently, to identify the main idea of that reading, and to be able to express their understanding in writing—or whatever other goal they have set out to accomplish. For most teachers, they really just need the data to see if they are moving closer to the goal or further away from that goal.

Collecting and analyzing data is not the end game itself; it is merely the means to the end. In the previous example, the teacher implemented DBQs to address a specific weakness in the state scores. To the teacher's dismay, when the scores came back he saw not the increase he expected, but an actual decrease!

How could this be? The students and the teacher had worked hard to address a weakness that was evident in the previous year's scores. Analysis of the new scores revealed that the students had indeed improved in their critical thinking, as tested by the state assessment. They had, however, gone down in the area of multiple-choice questions.

Multiple choice? But multiple-choice questions are not even the best means of assessing student knowledge! This is where reality breaks into theory. Even if a teacher holds the firm view that multiple-choice questions do not provide the appropriate level of assessment of student knowledge, and even if the research supports this view, the reality is that most state assessments contain multiple-choice questions. Like it or not, the state test is the measure by which schools are judged. The teacher was going to have to formulate a new plan.

Back to the drawing board? Throw out the previous strategy? Not so fast. The strategy the teacher put into place had indeed improved the students' skills in an area of documented weakness. Don't throw out the baby with the bathwater. How can the instruction in place be enhanced to also address the new area of concern?

Upon further reflection, the teacher remembered his concern about the lack of objective items on his assessments. As he observed his students, he realized that they had become very adept at skimming as they were reading. Skimming is a great reading strategy, however it is the worst strategy to use on multiple-choice items. Students were not reading carefully and were selecting the first response that contained a key word from the passage.

Instead of abandoning the DBQ component of his instruction, the teacher decided to supplement the document-based question with multiple-choice questions related to the same document. The teacher instantly discovered, after the first assessment, that his observation of students skimming instead of reading carefully was borne out in the results.

As a result of identifying, collecting, and analyzing teacher data, in conjunction with standardized tests scores, the teacher had developed a concrete plan to address an identified weakness on the part of his students.

Data analysis is a process. It is never the goal in itself. Once one area of weakness has been identified, addressed, and hopefully remediated, other weak areas will make themselves clear. Improvement is, by its very nature, an ongoing process.

This collecting and analyzing of data may seem like a lot of work, especially for teachers who have never analyzed scores deliberately before. The truth is that it does take a while, especially at the beginning. For most teachers, though, it is even more exhausting to spend hours and hours of time in the classroom implementing new strategies and never seeing the results when the state scores come back.

A great many teachers feel that they are teaching their hearts out and they see their colleagues doing the same thing. The problem is that the rest of the world doesn't see that. All the world outside of education sees are the state test scores and whether they are going up or going down. Like it or not, that is the measure of what schools are tasked to do, and if teachers are going to hit the target, they are going to have to get a lot more deliberate in their approach.

Another story: This one is not about classrooms, but about targets. Once upon a time in many rural communities, and in some still today, the fall was the season of the Turkey Shoot. Contrary to the title, no one was shooting at actual turkeys. That would have been a better test of skill. Instead, the participants fired a shotgun shell at a small paper target.

For those unfamiliar with shotguns, they shoot out a handful of small metal balls. The little metal balls, BBs, are aimed at a paper target with a bull's-eye printed on it. The person who has one of their BBs hit closest to the center of the bull's-eye wins a frozen turkey; hence the name Turkey Shoot.

This is not really much of a test of skill. Since nearly everyone hits the target, it happens to be very embarrassing to miss the target altogether. It is really kind of random chance who gets closest to the center. Many targets will have a dozen or more holes, with none in the center, while another target may only have one hole in the paper. Only one BB hits the paper, but that particular BB hits the target in the dead center. It isn't really about skill, but instead about dumb luck.

It may seem odd to have a story about rural entertainment in the middle of a book about how to improve teaching. It is rather odd, but there is something familiar in this story. Too many of those who are in the game of educational improvement are, in effect, throwing out a handful of pellets, hoping that one of them will hit the target.

This is not the kind of game that schools should be playing with students. There is too much on the line for teachers, students, schools, even the country. Schools should not just be flinging a whole bunch of different strategies at kids with the hope that one of them will work. Professional educators have to be entirely more deliberate.

Not only is throwing a whole bunch of strategies at the wall to see which one sticks a bad idea on the surface, but even success becomes a problem. If a whole bunch of strategies are used, how is anyone to know which one actually worked? It is impossible to have continued success in any endeavor if the cause of the success remains unknown.

Knowledge, as they say, is power. It is necessary to know what the goal is, what problem is keeping a particular teacher from reaching a goal. It is necessary to know what strategies might help individual students meet that goal and whether or not the use of those strategies is getting them there. Analyzing data may not be comfortable at first, but how else are teachers and schools going to get where they should be going?

The other side of the same coin is the way that educators incorporate the strategies that have proven to be successful into their regular practice. It seems that individual teachers are just as guilty as the systems they so often condemn.

Teachers complain bitterly about "flavor of the month" professional development and the "newest, latest" trends in education, but when a strategy really works, do teachers stick to it? How do teachers incorporate the new in with the old? The answer to this may also lie with the way in which teachers analyze their own data.

If classroom teachers are really looking at specific data, related to specific teaching strategies, over a significant period of time (a semester or more), then the tendency to abandon the new strategy should not be as great of a risk. When those who are implementing the new strategy can see the concrete results of that strategy, the new strategy is more likely to "stick."

This kind of specific focus on actual data is all too often lacking in classrooms or even in schools in general. It seems clear that if teachers take responsibility for their own personal research and back it up with their own data, they will have changed not only the outcome for their students, but also the way teaching happens. Professional development that actually causes teachers to develop as professionals, what a concept! (And it's the focus of the next chapter!)

Analyzing data is worthwhile in its own right. It does, however, have added bonus material. The kind of teaching that is described in this book is not revolutionary—nothing is really new—but it can be very different from what happens in the average classroom. Different can be a good thing, but it is almost always an intimidating thing at first.

Teachers often ask how to get administrators to "let" them teach this way. As it happens, most administrators don't worry so much about the way teachers teach, especially if students and parents are not complaining. However, if administrators do ask questions about any of the practices described in this book, teachers who have collected and analyzed their data will be able to show them the concrete data to back up what they are doing.

It is critical to have clear goals, in order for teachers to identify what problems are keeping them from reaching their goals. If teachers are identifying, collecting, and analyzing their own data, they will be able to develop deliberate strategies to address those problems and will have the data to back it all up.

As cool as data is, however, it is not a magic bullet. Neither collecting data, nor analyzing data will make students smarter or better prepared. Data does have the potential to keep teachers on the right track. It can help to make sure that the teacher in the classroom is not just throwing solutions at problems they don't even have. Teaching is a tough job, and time is short. There is not time to waste with strategies that don't work. Nor is there time to solve problems that don't even exist.

Teachers need to be clear about what they are doing, they need to identify the obstacles, and they need to know when they are making progress. Teachers need feedback, just as their students do, and an effective use of data can provide them with just that feedback.

KEY IDEAS TO REMEMBER

- Data analysis is critically important in determining the success, or lack thereof, of classrooms, schools, and districts.
- The key element in school improvement is to concentrate the energy on the problem. Good data analysis allows for the identification of the actual and not just the perceived problem.
- Once an area of concern has been identified, develop a strategy to address the concern. After the strategy has been implemented, it is critical to go back and look as objectively as possible at the data to see whether or not the strategy actually impacted the concern in a positive way.
- Data analysis is a process. It is never the goal in itself. The data is merely a tool, used by educators to ensure that the problem that is being remediated is indeed the actual problem.

QUESTIONS FOR FURTHER REFLECTION

- What data do you collect in your classroom/school? How do you use it?
- What issue or problem are you most concerned about in your classroom/school? What data have you collected to validate the problem?
- How would you measure the effectiveness of your current instructional focus? What data would help you to make this determination?

Chapter Eight

Professional Development That Gets Results

Up to this point, the focus has been on what happens in the classroom when the teacher shuts the door. It should be clear by this point that it is not enough to be attentive to one aspect of teaching, say curriculum, while ignoring another, like grading. All of the moving parts have to work together if schools are to break out and be genuinely effective.

If none of this information is new, if nothing really new is ever written about education, why aren't schools already universally high-performing? Is there some magic bullet out there that can turn the American educational system into the envy of the world? Probably not. Are there things that schools can do to drastically improve and become more effective? Absolutely!

Every teacher who reads this book believes, at least deep down, that education can be better, that schools can be more effective. If teachers did not believe this, they would have already given up, and they certainly would not be reading this book. Schools can get better than they are, and so can teachers. It is the interaction between students and teachers in classrooms that accounts for most of the time that is spent in schools, and so it is in classrooms, with teachers, that education will improve.

There is the belief, floating out in the air, as much hoped for as spoken, that teacher education, professional development, in-service programs, and the like will fix what is wrong in schools. This is certainly the sense one gets from the world outside of education. One of the first solutions that is put forward by state departments of education, politicians, and pundits is to spend more time and money on teacher training.

Teacher training really has two major components. The first is the training of new teachers at the undergraduate level. This is an extremely important factor in the effectiveness of classroom teachers, but it does not really fall within the scope of this book.

The focus here has been on what practicing teachers, in actual classrooms, can and should do to improve their teaching, how teachers can blend all of the best practices into a whole that gets the job done. The obvious key to this kind of improvement lies in professional development that focuses on helping existing teachers to make those connections.

All current and former teachers have extensive experience, up close and personally, with teacher professional development. In a great many places, teacher development is a mandated part of a school's budget each year. Schools everywhere have increased the time spent by teachers in meetings designed to improve teacher performance and thereby increase student performance.

With all this time and money spent, professional development for teachers should operate like a well-oiled machine. However, most teachers would say unequivocally that this is not the case. Many teachers view the in-service training they have been exposed to with a very jaundiced eye, and with good reason. Teacher development in too many places can be characterized as the "flavor of the month."

See if this sounds familiar. The week before school starts, teachers return to their districts and are greeted with the newest incarnation of professional development, or PD. Very often, this week before school starts is the first time that many of the teachers in the district have been introduced to the latest and greatest innovation to rock the world of education.

The seasoned teachers will groan and say that this new focus is the same thing the district did twenty years ago, only with a new name. The eager young teachers will listen attentively and worry that they will not be able to perform the task to the satisfaction of their evaluator. Many of the high-performing teachers will realize that this new task is something that they already implement, at least in part, in their classrooms. The low-performing teachers will seek out the back of the room and wait for this, too, to pass.

The new model will generally focus on one of the components of teaching that has been addressed here—usually only one component. It may be a focus on curriculum and new curricular materials. It may be a program with a long name shortened to initials: *RTI*, *PLC*, *DI*, etc. It may be based on a book or workshop that some district administrator read or attended at the end of the previous school year. Maybe it is a focus on a teaching tool like technology.

Sadly, many teachers can expect that this new program will be a major focus for the week before school begins, will still be talked about by a few conscientious teachers and administrators at Christmas, will be pushed to a back burner by spring, and will be replaced completely at the beginning of the next school year by a new program that will more than likely have no relation to the past year's program. Perhaps this should be called "flavor of the year," not "flavor of the month."

Is it any wonder then, that professional development of this type does not create lasting change in schools? It is an even greater tragedy that many of these programs were actually chosen by the teachers in the system. It's not that any one of these programs or areas of focus are inherently bad; it is just that the focus is too narrow—and it keeps changing.

Another familiar story: It is the last month of the school year and the professional development committee meets. This committee is usually made up of administrators and teachers and is tasked with providing professional development that is directed by and intended for classroom teachers. This group is faced with a daunting task: to choose a program that will meet every teacher's needs, address both the new and seasoned teachers, and fix the problem in the state test scores. This group, looking for a place to start, sends out a survey.

Nearly every teacher has completed this type of survey. It asks teachers what they would like to be developed in, for the coming school year. The better ones ask pointed questions to determine the level of proficiency of the staff, with questions like: *Rate your knowledge of XYZ program on a scale of one to ten*. The worst ones are completely open-ended and ask: *What would you like to be professionally developed in next year?*

The intention of the committee is laudable. They want to provide teachers with professional learning that will help teachers help students. They want teachers to buy in, and so the committee wants teachers to have some voice in the process. The reality is that if most teachers knew what they needed, they would already be doing it.

Teachers happen to be the most amazing individuals. When they see a problem, they nearly universally will jump to correct whatever needs correcting. If a teacher realizes that their classroom is lacking, they will spend endless hours of their own time, and often their own funds, to fill in the gaps.

A story to illustrate: A school decided to examine and increase the rigor of their teacher-made assessments. They passed out handouts with explanations of Depth of Knowledge levels. They passed out handouts with the DOK verbs so teachers could more easily create their own higher-level assessments. Teachers nodded their heads in understanding and agreement and nearly universally truly believed that their own assessments were in line with expectations.

Then someone on the leadership team had an idea. All of the teachers on the leadership team were asked to bring the most recent classroom assessment that they had used, or were about to use in their classroom. The school's best and brightest teachers sat down at a table with their very own assessments and were handed the same DOK chart.

Jaws fell open. These top teachers realized, almost instantly, that when they compared an actual assessment, one they themselves used in their own classroom, with the DOK chart, their assessments were almost completely lower-level questions. The instructive part of the story is this: Not one of those teachers had to be told to do anything.

Every one of those teacher leaders immediately went back and rewrote their assessments. Once the problem was clearly identified, they took the right steps to remediate the problem. That is what good teachers do.

The problem comes from the realities that are classrooms in the twenty-first century. Teachers juggle what sometimes seems like an endless array of expectations. They also confront the reality that every student, every classroom, every group of students that comes through the door is different and has correspondingly different needs.

The vast majority of classroom teachers do not have the time or the training to become proficient at taking all of the most current purely academic educational research and integrating that research into their daily lessons. Asking teachers what they need in professional development becomes a case of not being able to see the forest because of the trees. The responsibility for directing teacher professional development therefore falls on the shoulders of the building and district administrators.

Before everyone turns and points an accusatory finger at the nearest administrator, it would be wise to consider their preparation for this task. Just as teachers often scoff at their own undergraduate training as wholly insufficient to prepare them to actually teach students, so, too, administrators feel underprepared by their graduate training.

Graduate courses for administrators are not so different from the undergraduate courses that preservice teachers take. Teachers take courses that are designed to cover the gamut of all of the potential scenarios they could encounter. Administrative coursework is no different. Principals have to be ready for everything, from teacher evaluation to school safety issues. The training prospective administrators receive relative to teacher professional development is scant at best.

Administrators are therefore left to scramble and find some likely looking program to introduce to the staff. What ends up happening is that administrators get ideas from colleagues, books, workshops, etc., and without the time and training to thoroughly investigate what focus will move the building forward, a program is selected and the cycle starts anew. Plans that are not carefully and intentionally administered fall victim to the scenario described at the beginning of this chapter.

Even if the administrative/teacher PD team functions well, there is no guarantee that the PD that is offered will provide the kind of lasting change that modern schools require. Consider who serves on these administrative/

teacher teams. Usually these committees are made up of volunteers who have, if not a passion for, at least a solid interest in, PD.

These are the teachers who actively seek out the newest, latest, greatest ideas in PD. They have already read the book or attended a workshop. These go-getters, with the best of intentions, bring their latest discoveries to the table. An introduction is offered to the rest of the staff. The teachers on the committee launch into implementation, while the rest of the staff is still figuring out what the new program is all about.

The administrators on the committee are excited and looking for evidence of the new program in the classrooms they observe. The administrators who are not committee members are just as vague on the details as the majority of the staff.

As time and the school year pick up speed, the same routine happens again. Big focus on the new program at the beginning, still mentioning it at Christmas, lost in the shuffle of state testing in the spring, and on to another program for a new year as the year winds to a close.

The majority of the teachers on the staff are used to the routine. Many of them, sadly it seems, most especially the teachers who most need to improve, have learned to pay lip service to the new program. They implement some of the new ideas on the edges of current practice, and continue to do what they have always done. Even teachers who are thoughtful and want the program to succeed can become so acculturated to the PD process that they get bored if the focus does not change on a yearly basis.

The problem, of course, is that what has always been done often doesn't work very well. This kind of glancing blow at integrating new methodology results in an environment in which too many teachers never really understand the program from the outset. Even if teachers do understand the new program, the time that is actually spent putting the new into practice is not sufficient to move that practice from novelty to routine, and so no long-term change occurs.

This all sounds pretty dismal. Is there no hope for schools to change? Is education doomed to stay on the hamster wheel, just regurgitating the same old tired catchphrases forever? Why bother with professional development at all?

The point of this book is that there *is* hope. Schools can work and become the truly effective institutions that everyone is looking for. What's more, it turns out that professional development is, if not a magic bullet, at least a key factor in creating that change.

In order for professional development to be part of the cure instead of part of the problem, a few key understandings must be reached. First, no real, lasting, important change is going to happen overnight, or even in one school year. Second, just looking at one component of what goes on in school is not going to be enough; what goes on in schools is as multifaceted as it gets, and so the solution must also be multifaceted. Third, if this was easy, someone would already have fixed it. Lastly, improvement is a process, not an end product.

There are lots of ways to approach the development of a PD program that will actually create a better school, and no one way is necessarily any better than any other. It is at this point that many schools and even school districts turned to canned programs.

Canned programs are those professional development programs that offer a prescriptive process to improve schools. They are usually the by-product of some school improvement initiative that happened in some other system. It is not hard to see the allure of these programs. After all, this approach worked for the XYZ School and look at their scores. If another school just follows the pattern, they should have great results, too.

These canned programs are everywhere; some work better than others, but they all have the same pitfall. Too often schools use these kind of canned programs to take a shortcut. No one wants to spend a lot of time in building a program, especially all that time in meetings. If all the meeting time is cut out, the logic is, improvement will happen faster.

The draw of the program then becomes the weakness. What made that canned program work in the school in which it was developed in the first place was usually the collaboration that had to take place in the development of the plan. When a motivated group of educators comes together and identifies what they want their school to be like, examines the roadblocks to becoming the ideal school, and develops strategies to change, they have usually already accomplished most of the mission.

School change is hard. Schools are deeply imbedded institutions. Not only that, but everyone is an expert. After all, everyone went to school and so therefore everyone, not just the professional educators, has ideas about how to fix the schools. For real change to happen takes time and lots of conversation with lots of people to develop change that will be meaningful and lasting.

Instead of creating another canned program in the pages of this book, instead take a look at one school's journey to create meaningful professional development and examine what the thought processes were that led to the model they developed. It is not the program itself that is meaningful, but rather the rationale that went into the decisions that were made.

A large suburban high school in the middle of the United States—in the middle of its state's demographics for socioeconomic standing, per-pupil spending, teacher pay, and student achievement—wanted to improve. The school had, in the past, tried many of the canned programs that were in vogue at the time and found in each the same kind of limited results that kept the school in the middle of the middle.

The leadership team decided to put together their own professional plan. One of their first considerations was to develop a plan that would span more than one school year. They were sensitive to the complaints of teachers that the "flavor of the month" was leaving staff feeling as if they were just paying lip service to the latest plan.

The team also wanted a plan that was research-based. State guidelines required professional development to be based on proven, research-based strategies. In addition to the state mandate, the team did not feel that it would be necessary, nor even advisable, to reinvent the wheel. Seeking out the best research on effective strategies became the foundational work that led the rest of the process.

A final major consideration was also based on listening to teacher concerns, that the plan not be a one-size-fits-all model. Teachers, like the students they teach, are not all exactly alike. New teachers have different needs than experienced teachers. Teacher interests are different, and so the plan needed to be flexible enough to be differentiated for teachers.

Conversations among this leadership group then turned to the task of identifying the area of greatest concern for the building. They asked themselves and each other, "What one component in the life of the school could be improved to most significantly improve the teaching and the learning in the school and thereby student achievement?" Their conclusion was to focus on teaching strategies that would engage students in the learning. It seemed that too much of the average student's time was spent in passive listening and not in active engagement.

With these basic guidelines in place, the team started by seeking out the research-based teaching strategies that were widely available on the market at the time. Leaders among the administrative and teaching staff went to carefully selected conferences and workshops to first learn about the most current research available and to become knowledgeable enough about those strategies to bring them back to the staff.

The team divided itself into groups, and each group became "expert" in a particular strategy. Then the PD calendar for the year was set, with each of the "expert" groups taking responsibility to teach their teaching strategy to the entire staff. The groups were very deliberate in their effort to model their chosen strategy when teaching it to the staff. They believed that modeling the strategies for teachers not only helped teachers to understand the strategy better, but also underscored the value of the strategy itself.

The teams were comprised of teachers who were respected by their peers. This was considered essential, since teachers who did not enjoy the professional respect of their peers would not be seen as compelling. The teams also had administrators from the building. If the administrators were going to send the message that this was important, they needed to be visible in the process. They also needed to gain the expertise to recognize a successful use of the strategies in action.

In addition to modeling the strategy to the whole group, each of the "expert" groups was careful to provide teachers with handout materials containing concrete examples of sample lessons that teachers could use. These sample lessons intentionally encompassed every content area so that math teachers had math examples, business teachers had business examples, and so on. In this way, each teacher created a personal binder of materials to which they could refer later as they created their own lesson plans.

The leadership team felt that it was extremely important for teachers to have concrete resources to which they could refer as the year progressed. They very deliberately wanted each teacher to have this resource immediately available—in the teacher's hands and not stuck on some shelf in the school library where it would become just another forgotten binder.

The expectation for the whole teaching staff was that they would each incorporate at least one lesson, using the introduced strategy, into their teaching in the month after the strategy was presented. Time was also set aside in department meetings to discuss the successes and challenges that teachers faced as they implemented these new strategies.

At the end of the first year, the leadership team reviewed their progress and made plans for the next phase of professional learning. The key question that emerged was, *Why do teachers abandon new strategies, even when they are successful, in favor of more familiar but less effective strategies as the school year progresses?*

There are surely many explanations for this phenomenon, but the fact that it happens with nearly every new strategy that is introduced is clear. Perhaps one of the key reasons that using new strategies at the beginning of the year, but neglecting them as the year progresses is such a common occurrence has more to do with the nature of the school year than with the strategies themselves.

Most experienced teachers can find, stuffed into binders or file drawers, many examples of engaging classroom lessons that were used and then abandoned. Teachers often seem surprised when they come upon these lessons. They liked the lesson, the students enjoyed it, but somehow it was lost in the shuffle, stuffed in the drawer and forgotten. Most of the professional development that teachers have experienced leaves this kind of forgotten material in its wake. Why?

The answer may lie in the pace at which a school year moves. Each school year is really a self-contained entity. It has a clear beginning, middle, and end. Unless there is an intentional focus on acquiring the new strategy and incorporating it intentionally, it is likely to be used and then lost, just as when students cram for a test and then forget the material before the end of the year.

The beginning of a school year starts off at a relatively controlled pace. It picks up steam through the late fall and has a mini-climax at the end of the first semester, which in many systems falls at the Christmas break. Depending on the regional climate, the second semester may come in fits and starts as weather creates unexpected school closings. The middle and end of the second semester can become frenetic as teachers prepare for state testing, final exams, and the end of the school year.

Compare this progression to the implementation of new teaching strategies. At the beginning of the school year, teachers are fresh and willing, even eager, to implement new lessons and strategies. The pace picks up at about the time of parent-teacher conferences and other duties begin to encroach on a teacher's attention. Teachers start to retreat into strategies that are more familiar as their time to plan becomes more limited. The end of the year is a rush of getting things completed, leaving no time to think of new strategies.

Add to this the further complication of a new set of professional development foci at the beginning of each new year, and it is no wonder that the new strategies that teachers learn are too often left languishing in the drawer.

How then can good professional development combat the cyclical nature of a teacher's year in school? The reason that teachers seem to abandon the new in favor of the old is because the old is familiar. It is human nature to take refuge in the familiar in the face of stress. The only way that new strategies are going to really take hold is if they can be made familiar. That way, when teachers are scrambling for a lesson plan idea in February, the strategy that comes to mind may be a new one.

As the school in this example completed their first year of professional development, the shape of the second year began to emerge. They needed to find a way for teachers to choose a new strategy and use it with regularity throughout the length of a school year. Teaching strategies, like any new learning, need a certain amount of repetition to create familiarity and comfort. Teachers were going to need a structure that was supportive as they experimented with a new strategy. There was also a need for accountability to ensure that the new strategies were really being used on a regular basis.

The plan that was developed incorporated these considerations, along with the framework of learning communities and the introduction of data-driven decision-making.

Teachers were asked to choose the strategy that they wanted to be able to use with more confidence in their classrooms. They were asked not to choose a strategy that they already felt competent in. The teachers choosing a particular strategy were placed into groups with other teachers who also selected that same strategy, across grade levels and departments. Each group was assigned a teacher leader who would serve as facilitator.

In order to focus on the role of data, teachers were asked to identify a specific goal, with regard to student growth, that would be improved by the use of the strategy that they had selected. These goals had to be specific and measurable, and teachers were trained to establish benchmark scores for their students. Each teacher was also asked to commit to a schedule for the frequency of the use of the strategy.

Teachers were then asked to chart their students' scores at regular intervals over the course of the school year. The faculty groups met monthly to discuss their struggles and their successes as they implemented the strategy they had chosen to add to their regular instruction.

These groups were deliberately designed to be made up of teachers across grade levels and content areas. Going back to the discussion in Chapter 3, creating engaging classrooms is more a function of the *way* that a teacher teaches than it is the *content* that the teacher teaches. When teachers from differing subject areas met to discuss the strategies they were practicing in the classroom, the conversation could focus more on the use of the strategy than on the specific content.

This may sound contradictory when compared to the examples that teachers were given while they were learning the strategies the year before. The leadership team wanted each teacher to have some concrete examples of how to implement a specific strategy in a specific content area. This was so that teachers could learn the strategy to begin with, the same idea as "guided practice" in a bygone era.

In the groups, when teachers from different content areas met to discuss their successes and challenges, the discussion would be more focused on the strategy itself, and on teacher mastery of the strategy. Think of the discussion in Chapter 3 about how students often characterize their favorite teachers. It is the *way* teachers teach that engages students more than *what* the teacher teaches.

The staff met on a regular basis to compare what was working and what they were struggling with as they grew more proficient in implementing their chosen strategy. They also compared the data that they had been collecting to measure student achievement as a result of the implementation of the strategy. It turns out that helping each other with data collection and analysis was a bigger part of the group conversation than the strategy itself.

The format of this type of professional learning activity could be extended for as long as was deemed effective. As new needs, or new weaknesses, were identified by the school community, they could be integrated into this model.

The important takeaway from looking at a model like this is not to replicate this exact model. Instead, it is important for those directing professional development activities for teachers to be thoughtful in the way that those activities are chosen. This is certainly not meant to be a canned program!

Go back and reread Chapter 1. The program itself is not the key to success. Remember "Pizza on Tuesdays"? What makes a program successful and makes schools more effective is driven more by the collaboration of those involved in the program than in the actual program itself.

Now think about the professional development experiences that were described at the beginning of the chapter. It is no wonder that teachers have such a jaundiced view of PD. What makes good professional learning, learning that actually moves schools toward greater effectiveness? Good PD must be data-driven, and the strategies being taught need to match the identified needs of the school.

Teachers need time to practice, not just once at the beginning of the year, but often and with the support of others who are also invested in the new strategies. There should also be a recognition that not all teachers, like not all students, are in the same place in their learning. Good PD is differentiated to accommodate the needs of a wide range of teacher experience.

Most of all, for professional development to have any lasting impact it needs to be connected to itself. Continuing to pull random teacher behaviors for improvement, with no relation between them, is fruitless as well as frustrating. Teachers have to know, understand, and master all of the varied components of teaching simultaneously. Good curriculum for students is a spiral; good PD for teachers should do the same.

Professional development is ubiquitous in American schools. It is viewed by those outside the schools as the cure to ineffectiveness. Sadly, it is viewed by too many inside of those same schools as part and parcel of the problem. This does not have to be the case. Professional development that is thoughtful and targeted can indeed be a cause for good. The key is to approach PD as another one of the integral parts of teaching, and have it work to support the whole.

Professional development really is the culmination of everything that has been discussed. Once each individual teacher, and then the school as a whole, has reviewed their level of expertise in each of these areas, finding a specific area in which to focus professional development becomes less of a pin-the-tail-on-the-donkey kind of exercise. Just as the components of teaching need to be integrated to be most effective, professional development needs to be an integrated part of the program in effective schools.

KEY IDEAS TO REMEMBER

- Much of the professional development that is offered to teachers does not create lasting change in schools.
- Effective professional development must, like classroom teaching, be data-driven.

- Professional development is a key factor in creating real and lasting change in schools if it is targeted, ongoing, and creates an interconnected system.
- School improvement is a process, not an end product.
- Approach PD as another one of the integral parts of teaching, and have it work to support the whole.

QUESTIONS FOR FURTHER REFLECTION

- How does your building/district determine the professional development focus for a school year?
- What was the last major professional development activity in your building/district? How many teachers are still involved with this focus? What would increase this number?
- What data do you use in your building/district to choose a professional development focus? How do you measure the effectiveness of the teacher learning?

Chapter Nine

Putting It All Together to Get Results

With all of the educational literature available, anyone who has been engaged in the field of education for long has seen many trends come and go. Sit in any professional development activity with veteran teachers, and they will scoff and say that this new latest, greatest strategy is the same old, same old with a different name. As it happens, nothing in this book is particularly new or improved, either. Certainly the ideas represented here don't constitute a package or a program that will solve all the problems in any particular district, school, or even individual classroom.

Instead, this book is an attempt to share experiences from the classroom to the administrator's office and back to the classroom. To show how the meshing of theory and practice can improve the experience that teachers have. To show how teachers can maximize opportunities so that they can improve their classrooms and be more effective with their students. Not only do the theory and the practice need to mesh, but also the different parts of what teachers do, from curriculum to data, from August to May, need to mesh. So this is a good time to review all of the different ideas and see if they really do blend together to create a whole.

Synergy is defined as the interaction of two or more agents so that their combined effect is greater than the sum of their individual parts. Educators see this at work in education every day. A group of teachers who work together to solve a problem will come up with a solution that is better than any one of them could have achieved on their own. This is why teaming and learning groups have proven to be so popular and so effective. Pulling in a group of people with a common goal is a clearly a way to create the kind of synergy that gets problems solved.

Experienced teachers will recount, sometimes even with amazement, that individual classrooms have their own synergy. Add or take away just one or two key students and the whole atmosphere changes, for better or for worse. It doesn't seem, on the surface, that a class of twenty would be significantly different from a class of twenty-one, but if that one student is either a terror or a wonder, the class changes as a whole.

This is the one of the reasons that committee membership is so key. Take away one or two key individuals and the entire committee functions differently. Synergy is a real force in schools, but unfortunately it seems to be a force that isn't taken advantage of as often as it could be. This is especially true with the component parts of teaching itself.

In addition to individual personalities, there are a lot of moving parts involved in the work that happens in a school. Effective teachers understand that curriculum, instruction, assessment, grading practices, and data analysis are the components that must not only be present, but be high functioning, if a classroom is going to operate smoothly and efficiently.

Most master's degree programs specialize in only one of these areas; likewise, most of the educational literature focuses on only one of these areas. In the real world, where the teaching happens, effective educators must be able to harness all these components to find lasting success. Schools, like the students they teach, are not one-dimensional.

It is time to pool the collective knowledge of all the teachers in a building or district so that they can use the powerful force of synergy to maximize their efforts. Thinking about the whole, while working through the parts, seems obvious. Unfortunately, like so many things that seem obvious, it is not always automatic. Professional development must become the means by which the school improves, from the classroom out.

A truism in schools that is often shared with new employees in the school setting, teachers, assistants, administrators, or others, is that school doesn't really make sense until one has lived through a whole school year cycle. There are things that happen at the beginning of the year that don't necessarily make sense until the end. This may account for why change can be so slow to take root in the educational arena.

The difficulty seems to be in remembering all the parts as they work together. The good news is that each year provides educators with a fresh start. The bad news is that continuity can be very difficult to foster. Again, this is an area that professional development can facilitate by being thoughtful and targeted, instead of being random and piecemeal.

Curriculum is the starting place: What do the students need to know? The ability to merely identify the core ideas that students need to know is only the beginning, but as rudimentary as simple identification of core knowledge is, it is critical. As hard as it may be for those out in the forefront of educational reform to fathom, there are still large numbers of classroom teachers who struggle to articulate, beyond naming a chapter in a textbook, the key concepts that they want their students to know.

If teachers cannot articulate, very clearly, exactly what they want their students to know and be able to do, what chance is there that those same students will be able to master those concepts? Starting at the beginning may seem trite, but the role of a clear and teacher-friendly curriculum document or, at the very least, an outline that teachers develop for themselves to focus on the key curricular objectives, cannot be overstated.

In conjunction with curriculum itself, if there is no intentional plan on the part of the teacher for how that teacher is going to check for that "knowing" when the teaching is finished, then teachers can very easily leave off important pieces of the learning, or get too caught up in the minutia. This distracts students from a focus on what is key and leaves them feeling that learning is random.

Instruction is what teachers spend their days doing. Obviously teaching will happen in schools, but the quality of the instruction is the key for many students. The difference between students who are engaged versus students who are merely on task is often the key difference between those who succeed and those who fail. Instruction that engages students moves the action in the classroom from teaching to genuine student learning.

In addition to being engaged, if students are not provided with the right feedback at the right times, the teacher may not realize that the students didn't learn what was intended until it is too late to teach it again. Without feedback that is clear and targeted, students are left to feel that what happens in classrooms is out of their control and completely within the whim of the teacher.

Feedback is not only key to students, but also to teachers. Teachers need to have processes in place that give them an accurate picture of how the students have taken the material that was presented and internalized it at a level that will allow them to demonstrate that learning on teacher assessments as well as on the standardized, high-stakes tests that have become such a fixture in the modern educational landscape.

Teachers can assess and grade and collect mountains of numbers, but if they don't use that information to analyze their forward progress, they may not realize that no progress has been made. Not only does data give teachers information about the effectiveness of their teaching, it also has to inform the methods that teachers use. The scope of what is required in modern schools is too great for teachers to spend time remediating problems that they don't have. Data analysis is the only way to ensure that remediation is focused in the right place.

It is not enough to merely understand these very different areas of teaching in isolation. What is needed is to harness all of these seemingly disparate pieces so that the synergy that comes from all of the parts moving together can be realized. Teachers have to operate as an orchestra conductor who weaves the different instruments together so that a whole emerges.

Reminding teachers to take a big-picture look at what they do may seem obvious, but how often do teachers find themselves so caught up in one or another of those parts of being a teacher that they lose sight of the whole? How often does the professional development that is provided to teachers enhance the problem and not address solutions? It is not necessary that teachers be experts in all of these areas, but it is necessary to have a solid understanding not only of each area, but of how they operate together to create a whole.

This discussion started with the curriculum. Teachers must own it, not just read it. Gone are the days when schools can think that the table of contents of a textbook is the same thing as curriculum. Teachers must know, really know, and be able to articulate exactly what they want their students to know when they leave that classroom at the end of the course.

Just because an individual curriculum for the course(s) that are taught is written down, don't think that the objectives can't be manipulated. Teachers need to take curriculum guides down from the shelf, blow the dust off of them, and put them into a format that helps the teacher focus on what is really important. That's right, individual teachers need to remake those guides into genuine aids to their instruction! Think of the curriculum as a map: It is really hard for anyone to get where they are going if they don't know where "there" is.

Next, teachers need to think about what they can do, and more importantly what their students can do, so that the students will know those things that have been deemed important. What will help them to really make the content meaningful? Remember, if it is boring to the teacher, it will probably bore the students, too.

It is a tragedy to think about how much time students spend in school being absolutely, mind-numbingly bored. This statement may seem insulting, but there is just no other way to say it so that everyone will hear it. Now, this is not to say that every minute of every day can be wildly exciting; it doesn't even seem reasonable to think that it should be. If anyone has ever been with middle school students who are overstimulated, they will agree.

If, however, schools are to move beyond merely teaching, and into a place where students are genuinely learning, they simply must make teaching engaging, because that is, in fact, how learning really happens. Mere exposure to material is certainly not equivalent to actual learning.

Teachers need to consider what they do to provide students with the feedback they need to learn. Just watch how someone learns. If no one ever tells the learner that they are on the right track, or, more typically in schools, only waits until the learning is over to say that they have performed incorrectly, what would that individual have really learned? Does the feedback (read grades) that teachers provide really tell the story of what the young people in their classrooms know?

If learning is the goal, do the results (grades) reflect the learning that has happened? So often grades specifically, and feedback in general, have become the stick that schools use to prod the unwilling to do the things they are unwilling to do. This twists the results and leads to confusion, anger, and resentment—and this is just the way teachers react to grades! Think about what the goal of feedback really is. Unloading bad teacher habits in this area can be one of the most freeing things a teacher can do.

Question the results. Is there a plan to help students move forward? How does the teacher know the plan is working? If changing the approach to feedback is freeing, then getting intentional and concrete when it comes to the goals is real power. All teachers are collecting great mountains of data already. Successful teachers need to use some of that data to give themselves some feedback.

Often, teachers feel that they are like hamsters on a wheel. The expectations just keep coming, the students just keep coming, and the goals never seems attainable. The harder they work, the more things stay the same. If this sounds familiar, start using data to guide the work for positive results. Getting specific with goals, and using the data that is already being collected to measure progress, is a powerful way to get off the wheel.

All of these pieces are interlocking. Without a big picture, without synergy, schools just keep repeating the same pattern that everyone complains about. Teaching is an awesome profession for many reasons, not the least of which is the potential to always improve and grow. It is probably not possible to ever get as good as one can get in this job. There is always room for improvement and growth.

This is probably true in any job, but since the students are always changing, it seems even more true for educators. Teaching has been going on since Caveman #1 showed Caveman #2 how to make fire, or tools, or wheels. Even with all that history and experience, the human race still hasn't mastered all there is to know, much less how to teach that knowledge to others. It is the combination of research and experience that must guide schools forward.

Maybe teaching can't be "fixed," but it can certainly be made better than it is. Classroom teachers can take what research says works, get rid of some ideas that don't work anymore, and create classrooms where all students really do learn. Maybe there aren't any really new ideas; maybe it is all just rebranding of the same old stuff.

In the end it doesn't really matter if the ideas are old or new. What matters is that real teachers, in real classrooms, know what to do and then do it. There is enough information to do this thing the right way, but teachers need to stop just "doing" what has always been done and start thinking. Too many common teaching practices are holdovers that no one even realizes they have kept.

Take a look at what happens in the classroom. Look at the little things as well as the big things. If there is not a specific and thoughtful reason to keep doing something, it's time to let it go and move on. This is not a job for those who can only replicate what was done to them. This is a job that requires effective teachers to think all the time. Really effective teachers think about what they want to achieve and then put into place those practices that will move them to that goal.

A last analogy: Think about the art of teaching as the art of a weaver, the old-fashioned kind with a big loom. The framework of the loom is the curriculum; the shuttle (the part that takes the yarn back and forth) is the instruction. Effective teachers take their students back and forth, back and forth, and weave in the new ideas, the learning. When they are finished, there is a new product. It is not just a pile of yarn anymore. It is different from the materials from which it was made.

As weavers gain in skill, the cloth gets more interesting; the quality improves. This needs to be true in teaching, as well. As weavers grow in skill and confidence they incorporate their knowledge into a more intricate product. Skilled teachers take the best new ideas about how to teach and incorporate them into what they are doing in the classroom.

Each new school year gives educators the chance to create a new cloth. They weave in the new things they have learned, they try to avoid the mistakes that they made the last time, and they anticipate the problem areas. The important thing about the analogy of a loom is that it creates a whole, not a patchwork of added-on pieces, but a whole that is indistinguishable from its parts.

As teachers think about their classrooms, they need to think about the piece of cloth that they are trying to create. What should it look like when it is finished? What will it take to make it look like the model in their head? Teachers need to cultivate the ability to take all the best ideas they have learned and incorporate them into the design. Not all at once, but a little at a time so that when the teaching is finished, something infinitely valuable has been created.

KEY IDEAS TO REMEMBER

- Effective educators must be able to harness all of the components of teaching to find lasting success.
- Teachers must have and/or create a clear and concise working document detailing the content that is deemed essential for each course. It is critical that teachers can clearly articulate exactly what they want their students to know and be able to do.
- Student engagement in learning is the key goal of good instruction.

- All learners require accurate and timely feedback on their learning.
- A student's grades must reflect the progress that student has made toward mastery of the curricular goals. They must reflect learning, not be a catch-all that dilutes their impact.
- Collection and analysis of teacher-generated data by the teacher is the only way teachers are accurately able to adjust their instruction to improve.

QUESTIONS FOR FURTHER REFLECTION

- What implications of the synergy of the components of teaching do you see for your classroom/school after reading this book?
- What will you do differently to make your teaching more effective? Why?

About the Author

Ann Chase has been engaged in public education for twenty-seven years as a classroom teacher, a high school assistant principal, and back again in the classroom as a middle-school history teacher. She has taken the lessons of the classroom into administration and the lessons of administration back into the classroom, where she has successfully integrated the best practices from her book into her daily teaching.

www.ingramcontent.com/pod-product-compliance
Lightning Source LLC
Chambersburg PA
CBHW030147240426
43672CB00005B/303